The Single Market Review

IMPACT ON TRADE AND INVESTMENT

TRADE CREATION AND TRADE DIVERSION

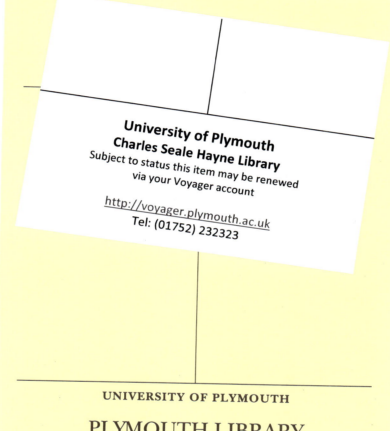

The Single Market Review series

EUROPEAN COMMISSION

The Single Market Review

IMPACT ON TRADE AND INVESTMENT

TRADE CREATION AND TRADE DIVERSION

The Single Market Review

SUBSERIES IV: VOLUME 3

OFFICE FOR OFFICIAL PUBLICATIONS
OF THE EUROPEAN COMMUNITIES

KOGAN PAGE . EARTHSCAN

This report is part of a series of 39 studies commissioned from independent consultants in the context of a major review of the Single Market. The 1996 Single Market Review responds to a 1992 Council of Ministers Resolution calling on the European Commission to present an overall analysis of the effectiveness of measures taken in creating the Single Market. This review, which assesses the progress made in implementing the Single Market Programme, was coordinated by the Directorate-General 'Internal Market and Financial Services' (DG XV) and the Directorate-General 'Economic and Financial Affairs' (DG II) of the European Commission.

This document was prepared for the European Commission

by

Centre for Economic Policy Research

It does not, however, express the Commission's official views. Whilst every reasonable effort has been made to provide accurate information in regard to the subject matter covered, the Consultants are not responsible for any remaining errors. All recommendations are made by the Consultants for the purpose of discussion. Neither the Commission nor the Consultants accept liability for the consequences of actions taken on the basis of the information contained herein.

The European Commission would like to express thanks to the external experts and representatives of firms and industry bodies for their contribution to the 1996 Single Market Review, and to this report in particular.

Office for Official Publications of the European Communities
2 rue Mercier, L-2985 Luxembourg
ISBN 92-827-8798-2   Catalogue number: C1-70-96-003-EN-C

Kogan Page . Earthscan
120 Pentonville Road, London N1 9JN
ISBN 0 7494 2332 3

Table of contents

As well as the technical appendices listed above, there are detailed supplementary appendices describing results by country and by industry with respect to each of the methodologies employed in this study. The key results from these appendices are summarized and discussed in the main body of the text. Listed below is the information which is included in these supplementary appendices, which are not published in the report but which are available on request from the authors.

Supplementary appendices to Chapters 3, 4, 5

Exchange rates
Growth rates
Coverage ratios – France
Actual and adjusted changes in trade shares – 2-digit NACE
Table A.4.D. Estimation results for demand equations
Table A.4.P. Estimation results for price equations
Table A.4.S. Summary of SMP demand and competition effects
Table A.5.1. Ex-ante simulation
Table A.5.2. Ex-post simulation with no direct external effects
Table A.5.3. Ex-post simulation with direct external effects
Table A.5.4. Integrated markets simulation
Table A.5.5. Comparison of methodologies

List of tables

List of figures

List of abbreviations

BIL	Buigues, Ilzkovitz and Lebrun
BLEU	Belgo-Luxembourg Economic Union
CGE	Computable general equilibrium
Comext	Database of external trade statistics (Eurostat)
CSO	Central Statistical Office
ERM	Exchange rate mechanism
EU	European Union
Eurostat	Statistical Office of the European Communities
GDP	Gross domestic product
IMF	International Monetary Fund
NACE	General industrial classification of economic activities within the European Communities
OECD	Organization for Economic Cooperation and Development
RoW	Rest of the world
SMP	Single market programme
VAT	Value added tax
VISA	Variables for Industrial Structural Analysis

Acknowledgements

This is the final report of a study on 'Competitiveness impacts and the quantification of trade creation and trade diversion due to the Internal Market programme' undertaken by the Centre for Economic Policy Research for the European Commission.

The study was undertaken by Christopher Allen (University of Maastricht), Michael Gasiorek (University of Sussex), and Alasdair Smith (University of Sussex).

The authors are grateful for the research assistance of Yusaf Akbar and Ulrike Hotopp, for the comments and advice of Peter Holmes, Paul Brenton, Daniel Gros and several members of staff of the Commission's services, and for the co-operation of Bruce Lyons in making available to us a pre-publication copy of *Industrial Organization in the European Union* and electronic copies of his data.

1. Summary

1.1. The nature of the study

The subject of this study is the competitiveness impacts and the quantification of trade creation and trade diversion effects due to the single market programme (SMP).

The SMP was expected to expand trade among European Union (EU) partners as they remove trade barriers with each other. Increased trade among partners could be at the expense of trade with third countries; or on the other hand the SMP could have the effect of improving market access for third country imports into the EU market. A major objective of the SMP was that increased competition within the EU should reduce the costs for EU producers and make them more competitive with non-EU producers, which in turn would affect trade patterns. Thus, in broad terms, in this study we are looking at the different ways in which the SMP could affect trade patterns, both within the EU and between the EU and its trading partners.

'Trade creation' and 'trade diversion' refer to the direct effects of changes in intra-EU trade barriers on intra-EU and extra-EU trade, while 'external trade creation' refers to the possibility that changes in the accessibility of the EU market to non-EU imports could increase extra-EU trade. These are economic concepts which are generally uncontroversial, with the analysis giving rise to clear predictions, and the research question being principally the empirical problem of identifying what have been the actual effects of the SMP. By contrast, the notion of 'competitiveness' is controversial, and much less clearly defined; and since changes in competitiveness will induce changes in wages and in exchange rates, the predicted effects on trade patterns are not unambiguous, so it is less clear what is being looked for empirically.

1.2. Research methods

We employ three research approaches. The first is based on descriptive statistics of trade patterns. At the two-digit sectoral level we study coverage ratios, the ratios of exports to imports in both intra-EU and extra-EU trade for individual EU countries; and we also undertake market share analysis at the same sectoral level for the EU as a whole, describing how demand for the products of a sector is divided between domestic products, imports from other EU countries, and imports from non-EU countries.

The second approach is econometric. The econometric model uses data from 15 sectors at the three-digit level together with some macroeconomic variables to study two interconnected relationships – the forces determining the allocation of market demand between home producers, other EU producers, and non-EU producers, and the influences on pricing. The econometric approach assumes producers behave in an imperfectly competitive fashion, selling goods differentiated from those of their competitors. The allocation of demand is modelled as depending on income and on prices of goods from different sources, while price is modelled as a function of costs and competition. Systematic changes in demand from 1992 onwards, which cannot be accounted for after controlling for the effects of prices and income, are attributed to changes in trade barriers between markets; and systematic changes in pricing, after controlling for costs and competition, are attributed to changes in the competitiveness of producers.

The third approach is based on a computable general equilibrium (CGE) model. It, too, operates at the three-digit level, but with more comprehensive sectoral coverage, and it, too, models producers as imperfectly competitive firms operating in markets with differentiated products. The CGE model is more elaborate than the econometric model, allowing a richer set of linkages between markets (notably linkages between sectors through the labour markets), but whereas the parameters of the econometric model are estimated on the basis of data series spanning several years, the parameters of the CGE model are imposed, some on the basis of estimates from the literature, and the rest so that the numerical solution of the model reproduces the data of a single base year. One exercise undertaken with the CGE model is an ex-ante simulation, where estimates made in 1990 of the likely effects of the SMP on intra-EU trade costs are imposed on the model and the effects on the equilibrium recomputed. The second kind of exercise undertaken is an ex-post simulation, where the values of the changes in trade costs are chosen so as to reproduce as an equilibrium the changes in market shares observed between 1991 and 1994. We make alternative assumptions in the simulations about the effect of the SMP on trade costs, to investigate the extent to which the SMP may have affected external trade barriers. We also investigate the properties of a simulated equilibrium in which firms pricing behaviour does not respond to changing market shares, in an attempt to isolate what the model has to say about the effects of competition.

The different research approaches offer different approaches to the problem of the counter-factual – the comparison we wish to make is not between EU markets before and after the SMP, but between EU markets after the SMP and how EU markets would have behaved if the SMP had not happened. In a changing world, it is difficult to make a clear separation between the effects of the policy change being studied and the effects of other changes which would have taken place in any event, that is to say, it is difficult to define a clear and agreed counter-factual.

The descriptive statistical approach offers an essentially informal answer to the problem of the counter-factual. The reader is presented with statistics and charts and is invited to make his or her own implicit or explicit judgements about the counter-factual. This approach has the obvious weakness of leaving interpretations to the subjective judgements of the reader, and is perhaps best thought of as a way of identifying hypotheses for more systematic investigation.

The econometric model is based on residual imputation: the variables included in the model are the ones which construct the counter-factual – everything else is attributed to the SMP. Any non-SMP effects which are wrongly omitted from the econometric model are falsely attributed to the SMP.

The ex-ante CGE model is an analytical approach which counts as SMP effects only those which result from variables which are chosen to represent the effects of the SMP. Its weakness is the mirror image of that of residual imputation: any SMP effects omitted in error from the model are not picked up in the estimates.

By contrast, the ex-post CGE approach returns to residual imputation, but with a counter-factual that is the pre-SMP trade pattern, so essentially attributing all changes to the SMP.

1.3. Results of the descriptive statistics

Given the multiplicity of influences on trade balances and the theoretical slipperiness of the idea of competitiveness, it is perhaps unsurprising that investigation of coverage ratios at the two-digit level throws up several interesting observations but fails to provide unambiguous evidence of the effects of the SMP on trade patterns. The analysis suggests that:

(a) The different experiences of different countries suggest that there have been changes in competitiveness which cannot be attributed solely to exchange rate effects or to other macroeconomic influences.

(b) Inter-sectoral differences within countries are similarly sufficiently large to imply that there were microeconomic, sectoral influences on competitiveness, as well as exchange rate and other macroeconomic factors.

(c) There seems little evidence of common patterns of changes in sectoral competitiveness across countries, except in sectors where the changes seem to derive from long-run structural change, independent of the SMP.

Our investigation of the importance of competitiveness effects on trade is suggestive rather than conclusive. At best, therefore, the analysis of coverage ratios identifies questions worth investigating further, rather than giving clear answers to these questions.

By contrast, changes over time in consumption shares seem to be less vulnerable to short-term macroeconomic influences and as a result display patterns that are more informative:

(a) Market share analysis provides clear evidence that the change in the measurement of intra-EU trade in 1993 has had quite a strong effect on the statistics.

However, making what seems a reasonable allowance for the likely scale of measurement error introduced, still leaves considerable evidence of systematic changes in the patterns of intra-EU and extra-EU trade resulting from the SMP:

(a) In most sectors, EU markets have become increasingly open to imports from the rest of the world, with changes in the 1990s being the continuation of a longer-run trend.

(b) Several sectors show an increasing pace of extra-EU import penetration, so either the SMP or other changes in the 1990s have increased the openness of markets to extra-EU imports as well as intra-EU imports.

1.4. Econometric results

Our econometric estimates indicate the following:

(a) The single market has been trade-creating, both for EU and non-EU producers. There is little evidence of any substantial trade diversion of non-EU trade.

(b) After allowing for other influences on trade patterns, the average domestic market share has fallen by 5.4% in the 15 sectors studied, and by 2.2% in manufacturing as a whole. EU and non-EU producers have gained from this roughly in the same proportion, averaging across sectors.

(c) In some sectors, there has been a major expansion of EU import share with very little gain by non-EU producers. In contrast, large non-EU producer gains, sometimes at the expense of EU importer share, has been experienced in a second set of industries.

(d)   The SMP has also improved competitiveness: on average, after allowing for other influences on pricing, price-cost margins have fallen by an average of 3.9% since 1991 across the 15 sectors studied, and this fall is observed in all but one of the sectors studied. In manufacturing as a whole, there is a similar reduction. Some industries appear to have chosen to reduce prices rather than lose market share, while in other sectors, large falls in home market share are accompanied with only small falls in price-cost margins.

To examine the overall impact of the single market on trade flows, we need to consider the estimated direct effects on trade flows together with the further impact on trade flows of the estimated reductions in price-cost margins within EU countries. The competitive price-cutting response of home firms should, to some extent, restore the loss of market share caused by the direct effect of the SMP. Our estimates imply that:

(a)   on average, improved competitiveness adds an extra 1.2% to domestic market shares in the 15 sectors, roughly one quarter of our estimate of the average direct market loss;

(b)   intra-EU imports lose more market share than extra-EU imports as a result;

(c)   the overall impact of the SMP on trade flows is therefore an average loss of 4.2% in domestic market shares in the 15 sectors, with the gains divided almost equally between EU and non-EU imports, while for all manufacturing, the loss of domestic market share is 2.3%, with most of the gain going to non-EU imports.

1.5.   CGE results

Simulation of the CGE model using ex-ante estimates of the direct effects of the SMP based on the study of Buigues, Ilzkowitz and Lebrun [1990], necessarily produces the result that intra-EU trade grows at the expense of home market shares, and to a lesser extent at the expense of extra-EU imports. However, the actual changes in trade patterns between 1988 and 1994 are quite different from those produced in these simulations: in many sectors there have been reductions in intra-EU trade (even after generous allowance is made for the effects of the statistical reporting change). The pattern across sectors of the magnitude of trade changes is different from that predicted by the model. The implication is that:

(a)   there have been more influences on the trade pattern than a simple reduction in intra-EU barriers;

(b)   it seems very likely that the sectoral distribution of the effects of the SMP has been quite different from that expected in advance.

Ex-post CGE analysis provides further evidence that the sectoral distribution of the effects of the SMP is different from that expected in 1990; it also suggests that there have been liberalizing forces on external trade that are at least as strong as the intra-EU effects of the SMP.

This could be interpreted as meaning that the SMP has caused external liberalization, perhaps because of the market access effects of having a single regulatory system, or explicit rules about public procurement. Alternatively, it could be interpreted as meaning that the SMP has been accompanied by external liberalization.

A full comparison of CGE results with econometric results is not possible because the econometric analysis covers only a limited range of sectors, but comparisons of the competition effects derived from the two approaches shows the econometric estimates of these effects being significantly greater than those derived in the CGE model, suggesting that there may be stronger competition effects from the SMP than are allowed for in standard numerical models based on imperfect competition.

Given that the different forms of analysis have different strengths, it is particularly interesting that both the econometric and the CGE analysis imply that:

(a)   the liberalization of external trade has been at least as strong as the intra-EU liberalizing effects of the SMP;

(b)   concerns about 'fortress Europe' effects of the SMP were unnecessary: the SMP has not in itself closed the EU market to third countries, nor has it been accompanied by protectionist measures.

2. Introduction and methodology

2.1. The nature of the study

The terms of reference for the study refer to the important implications for the terms of trade and trade policy of the removal of non-tariff barriers and the completion of the single market. 'On the one hand, the Internal Market was expected to expand trade amongst the partners as they remove trade barriers with each other (trade creation). On the other, [reflecting] the relative importance of remaining external trade barriers, [there] could also be expected [to be] increasing trade amongst partners at the expense of trade with third countries (trade diversion).' Perhaps with some time-lag, dynamic effects could generate further trade creation and trade diversion. The terms of reference also refer to the possibility of external trade creation, as common barriers against third countries are lower than the ones applied by the EU's partners.

Since there can therefore be changes both in trade flows and in the competitive position of European firms in relation to external competitors, 'on the one hand, the study should conduct an analysis of the impacts of competitiveness of European business in world markets. On the other, the study should determine in an analytical, quantitative way whether the Internal Market programme has result[ed] in greater trade, distinguishing between intra and extra-EU trade, and, therefore, assess the trade creation, trade diversion or external trade creation that has actually taken place'.

The terms of reference envisage that the analysis of the change in the competitive position of European firms in international markets 'should be analysed through a series of quantitative and qualitative indicators or proxies of structural factors determining competitiveness and the global performance of European firms'. Then 'a more analytical approach should be considered with a view to quantifying the impact of the Internal Market programme in relation to trade creation/diversion. No single ex-post model of trade impact will generally be able to consider the full range of factors and their interactions. [The project could be based on] several alternative models and/or methods and should study the internal coherence of results in order [to] obtain a sound final assessment'.

The underlying conceptual framework in which the nature of these different effects are discussed is presented in the remainder of this chapter together with an account of the different methodologies employed. Technical details of the research methods are included in the Technical Appendix to Chapter 2.

The analysis of changes in the competitiveness of European producers is presented in Chapter 3, based on descriptive statistics of changing trade patterns which are presented in detail in the unpublished Supplementary Appendix to Chapter 3.

In the analytical[1] work, we have indeed adopted two radically different approaches, an econometric model presented in Chapter 4, and a computable general equilibrium (CGE)

---

[1]   Note that the term 'analytical' is used here, as in the terms of reference, to draw a distinction between formal modelling and descriptive statistics, whereas in Chapter 1 it was used, in the standard terminology of the literature on economic integration, to make a distinction between two methods of modelling counter-factuals.

model presented in Chapter 5. The methodological relationship between the two is discussed later in this chapter.

2.2. The conceptual framework

Baldwin and Venables [1995] present the development of the theoretical and empirical literature on the effects of integration on trade, production and welfare as taking place in three phases. A schematic outline is shown in Table 2.1.

Table 2.1.   The conceptual development of the economics of integration

Traditional approach	Tariff barriers
	Terms of trade effects
	Non-tariff barriers
Imperfect competition	Competition
	Scale
	Variety
Growth	Saving, investment, technical progress

The first phase was based on the traditional model in which international trade derives from comparative advantage in perfectly competitive markets. It classified the effects of tariff changes associated with integration into categories such as trade creation and trade diversion, and later extended into analysis of changes in non-tariff barriers and in the terms of trade. The second phase brought in imperfect competition and economies of scale: introducing the 'competitive effect' or 'profit effect' associated with changes in the output of goods on which price is not equal to average cost, the 'scale economy' effect associated with changes in firm output, and the 'variety effect' when the number of varieties sold in any sector changes. The third phase introduced the dynamics of the effects on integration on saving, investment and economic growth. The different approaches are complementary rather than opposed to one another.

Historically, the first phase embodies the tools developed from the 1950s onwards by Viner [1950], Meade [1955], Johnson [1962] and others. This traditional theory of customs unions was grounded in the perfectly competitive model of international trade with the focus on the direct effects on prices of changes in trade barriers. The traditional approach recognized that there could be secondary effects (sometimes mistakenly referred to as dynamic effects), but a satisfactory treatment of such effects became possible only after the development in the late 1970s of models of trade with imperfect competition by Krugman, Helpman and others – see Helpman and Krugman [1985], for example. The 'dynamic' effects in the third phase arise from the analytical developments of the 1990s, stemming from the work of Romer [1986], Lucas [1988], and others.

The traditional literature originally focused on changes in tariff barriers, but the essence of the single market programme (SMP) is that it concerns primarily changes in non-tariff barriers. Baldwin and Venables [1994, 1995] show that the important distinction from the viewpoint of welfare analysis is not precisely that between tariff and non-tariff barriers, but between barriers which generate rents for the barrier-imposing country (tariffs and domestically-allocated quotas) and those which do not generate rents (voluntary export restraints and other exporter-allocated quotas, border and regulatory barriers which impose real costs). The significance of this distinction will be illustrated by example in the next section. However, in this study, our focus is on the positive effects of integration on the pattern of production and trade rather than on welfare analysis, and for us the distinction between rent-generating and non-rent-generating barriers is therefore of secondary importance.

Although the economics of non-tariff barriers can thus be analysed within a modified version of the traditional approach, much of the discussion of the SMP has focused on the likely effects of such barriers on competition, notably the way that regulatory differences and public procurement practices can facilitate market segmentation (Smith and Venables [1988], for example). Consideration of non-tariff barriers therefore draws us into analytical approaches based on imperfect competition.

Economists have different degrees of confidence in our analysis of the different approaches: generally speaking, our confidence declines as we move through the phases (down the rows of Table 2.1). The concrete, traditional analysis of the effects of tariff barriers involves policy changes of known magnitude and analytical methods (often simple supply-and-demand analysis) that are robust; terms of trade changes are not always easy to measure; analysis of non-tariff barriers (as in the single market programme) involves policy changes of less certain magnitude; the estimation of price-cost margins in imperfectly competitive industries involves inference from a body of theory in which there is no single accepted model of behaviour; the extent of scale effects is controversial; variety effects are generally accepted to be important but lack an agreed theoretical treatment; while, finally, endogenous growth effects are of very uncertain form and size.

Uncertainties notwithstanding, each element of the analysis is of potential importance in the understanding of the economics of integration. Reductions in non-tariff barriers such as regulatory costs on cross-border transactions are at the core of the SMP, and the direct effect of such changes is the natural starting point of analysis of the programme. But changes in external trade policy are associated with some aspects of the programme, and, in many markets, terms of trade effects can be important. Turning to the second set of effects: the central purpose of the SMP is to remove regulatory obstacles to competition, allow firms to expand their markets without monopolizing them, and enlarge the variety of choice available to consumers. Finally, the SMP should make the EU a more attractive base for both home and foreign investment, by providing a more predictable and uniform regulatory environment as well as improved market access, so there are potentially important effects in the third category too. Indeed, it is arguable that while our confidence in our understanding of the different effects declines as we move through the different phases of analysis, the empirical importance may well be increasing: the traditional triangles of consumer surplus and profit being commonly estimated to be smaller than the effects of scale and competition, and even modest effects on growth rates to be likely to have larger effects on income in the long run than static one-off changes.

The historical development of the analysis was also reflected in the empirical literature which, until the mid-1980s, almost entirely focused on estimating the direct effects and, in particular, trade creation and trade diversion (see, for example, Winters [1984]). Empirical analysis that introduced imperfect competition in a systematic fashion started with Cox and Harris [1985] and includes Smith and Venables [1988], and several of the chapters in Winters [1992]. Only recently, with Baldwin, Forslid and Haaland [1995] for example, has empirical analysis of integration included endogenous dynamics.

In this project our approach is empirical, and the available methods are not of a kind that allows us to distinguish finely between the importance of the different influences of integration on trade and production patterns, but it is nevertheless necessary to have an understanding of the different ways outlined above, in which the reduction of internal trade barriers associated with the SMP might impact upon patterns of production and trade. We employ a variety of research methods, and to understand the relative contribution of each to assessing the impact of the SMP on trade and production, it is necessary to understand how each method deals with the different effects outlined in this chapter.

2.3. The effects of integration on trade

Much of the standard empirical analysis of the effects of integration focuses on the changes in consumption shares in any given market. For any given EU country, total domestic consumption is divided between three sources of supply. The share of domestic production in domestic consumption (Home), the share of imports from the EU in domestic consumption (M_{EU}), and the share of imports from the rest of the world in domestic consumption (M_{RoW}) must, of course, sum to unity. Table 2.2 categorizes the traditional analysis of the different effects of integration on trade patterns in terms of impacts on these shares. A blank entry implies no change in the share, a positive sign an increase, and a negative sign a decrease.

Table 2.2. Direct effects of economic integration

Case	Description	Home	M_{EU}	M_{RoW}
1	Trade creation	-	+	
2	Trade diversion		+	-
3	External trade creation	-		+
4	External trade diversion		-	+
5	Trade suppression/erosion	+		-

If the reduction of trade barriers within the EU leads to imports from a partner country replacing local production, this is called (internal) trade creation and we have the changes in shares shown in the first row of the table, while the second row corresponds to the case where the lowering of internal trade barriers leads to imports switching from third country to partner country sources, i.e. (internal) trade diversion.

In the traditional analysis (internal) trade creation is welfare increasing: less efficient domestic production is replaced by more efficient partner country imports; while (internal) trade diversion is welfare reducing as higher-cost partner country imports replace lower-cost rest-of-the-world imports because of the discriminatory liberalization.

In the previous section, we noted that the welfare implications of changes in the real costs of intra-partner trade or in non-tariff barriers may be different from those of changes in tariff barriers. Consider one example to illustrate the significance of the distinction. Suppose the home country is importing a good, subject to a non-discriminatory tariff, from a third country whose cost is lower than that of the partner country. Discriminatory tariff removal with the partner country may lead to the good now being imported from the high-cost partner, and the rise in the cost of supply of imports (which will show up as a loss of tariff revenue) is income-reducing 'trade diversion'. By contrast, if the initial trade barriers took the form of voluntary export restraints in which the high domestic price is passed on to the exporter, then the discriminatory liberalization has the effect of reducing the cost of imports to the home country, even though the new source of supply has higher production costs than the initial source. The cost of imports falls, and there is no offsetting loss of tariff revenue.

However, our focus in this report is on the positive rather than the normative effects of changes in trade barriers and the traditional categorization of effects remains a useful taxonomy, even if the traditional welfare conclusions are no longer robust.

The last three lines of the table refer to the effects of integration on external trade barriers. Integration could reduce such trade barriers, for example if a shift from free trade area to customs union led to the implementation of a low common external tariff in a country that formerly had high tariffs, and this could give rise to external trade creation and diversion, as domestic production and partner imports, respectively, are replaced by foreign imports. On the other hand, the erection of high external barriers could have the reverse effect to external trade creation, i.e. trade suppression.

One possible effect of the SMP is the market-access effect analysed by Smith and Venables [1990]: the unification of regulatory systems within the EU may make EU markets more accessible to foreign producers, so giving rise to external trade creation. On the other hand, some American commentators have feared that unification of European regulatory systems could take forms that would increase discrimination against non-European suppliers, so suppressing external trade.

Given the difficulty of obtaining firm information on external trade barriers, it is difficult to distinguish in practice between trade pattern changes arising from the external effects of changing internal barriers (such as trade diversion) and those arising from changing external barriers (such as external trade diversion).

We can categorize the possible impacts on trade patterns from the competition, scale and dynamic effects of integration in the taxonomy of Table 2.2, even though that taxonomy was developed in the traditional customs union theory. However, the newer theories introduce further effects to be considered. The distinction between segmented and integrated markets is significant for the impact of integration under imperfect competition on the pattern of trade.

When there is national market segmentation, firms set prices in each national market independently. Integration will generate increased intra-union trade as internal liberalization cuts price-cost margins within the EU and leads to larger scale production by fewer firms. The creation of intra-industry trade need not generate increased net imports, as increased gross imports in any one sector for a particular country could be more than matched by increased gross exports to partner countries in the same sector.

However, if integration is accompanied by a switch to market integration in which producers treat the EU market as a single market in which they have to adopt a unified pricing strategy, the reduction in price-cost margins across the EU makes partner-country markets relatively less attractive than they are under market segmentation, so there will be less intra-industry intra-union trade: the effects on trade creation will be negative. Here again we have an example where the welfare effects of trade change are different from the traditional analysis: intra-EU trade is being reduced rather than created, but the impact of increased competition on national income will be positive.

There is less ambiguity about the trade diverting effects: both with segmented and integrated markets, the competitiveness of EU-based producers is likely to generate trade diversion as foreign-based producers lose market share in EU markets. The cutting of price-cost margins and the increased size and decreased cost of surviving firms are forces which will affect foreign as well as EU firms, but the effects will almost surely be stronger for EU firms which sell a larger share of their output to EU markets.

Turning finally to dynamic effects, if integration leads to increased income in the EU and therefore to increased saving and investment (Baldwin [1990], Ben David [1993]), trade with both partners and non-partners should increase, but not at the expense of domestic production. There seems no reason to suppose that dynamic effects will give rise to any particular pattern of change in consumption shares, and indeed it is plausible that different patterns would be observed in different sectors as endogenous growth leads to expansion of capital-intensive and high-technology sectors and decline of low-skilled and low-technology sectors.

2.4. Research methodologies

We employ three different approaches to investigate the effects of the SMP on patterns of trade and production. These are three quite distinct methodologies, and in order to make the most of their results, it is necessary to understand the relationship between them.

In the next chapter, we develop an approach based entirely on descriptive statistics. In order to keep the processing of information to a manageable level we operate at the two-digit NACE level in this part of the work. The focus is on making sense of the notion of 'competitiveness' and in that chapter we discuss the controversial nature of the concept. Consumption shares (import penetration ratios) for each two-digit sector are derived, describing how demand is divided between domestic products, imports from other EU countries, and imports from non-EU countries. To focus entirely on the sources of domestic consumption would, however, be to ignore what might be deduced about 'competitiveness' from the destinations of domestic output, so we also present statistics on intra-EU and extra-EU coverage ratios – the ratios of exports to imports.

An entirely descriptive approach cannot distinguish between the different sources of changes in trade patterns, so effectively all the different effects analysed above are in principle included in the statistics. Unfortunately, so also are any impacts on trade patterns arising other than from the SMP, and it is quite evident that macroeconomic variables such as exchange rates and differences in national growth rates have affected trade patterns. To take these descriptive statistics as a definitive indicator of the effects of the SMP would be to assume a counter-factual in which there were no macroeconomic or other effects on trade and production patterns. We can make informal guesses about the relative importance of SMP effects and other effects by comparing the experiences of different countries and different sectors, but the main value of the descriptive statistics is to pose questions and set an agenda for more systematic work.

As we turn from the descriptive work of Chapter 3 to the analytical methods of the later chapters, the conceptual focus shifts from 'competitiveness' to 'competition' effects. The SMP was expected to make a significant impact on the structure of markets by encouraging intra-EU competition which would induce more competitive behaviour by firms, with changes in the scale and possibly the number of firms driving down both costs and price-cost margins. These 'competition' effects should have positive effects on 'competitiveness', that is on EU firms' position in international markets, but given the difficulty of getting meaningful measures of competitiveness, the analytical modelling focuses directly on measuring effects on and of competition.

The econometric approach adopted in Chapter 4 seeks to make a clear distinction between the 'direct' effects and the 'competition' effects of the SMP by adopting a two-equation approach in a model of imperfect competition between firms operating in markets for differentiated products. In the equation for market shares, price and income variables are included as conditioning variables so that the single market dummy variable should pick up changes in the allocation of demand between domestic products, imports from other EU countries, and imports from non-EU countries, which cannot be explained as reactions to income or price changes. The effects of the single market on price-cost margins are picked up by the pricing equation in which the conditioning variables control for labour and materials costs, for competitors' prices and market shares.

Methodologically, therefore, the modelling of Chapter 4 can be seen in simple terms as seeking to filter out other effects on trade patterns so that only unexplained changes are attributed to the SMP – it is essentially a 'residual imputation' model. Inevitably, the effects of excluded variables are in danger of being mistaken for those of the SMP.

The computable general equilibrium (CGE) approach of Chapter 5 is based on the same economic ideas – imperfect competition with product differentiation – but with a radically different modelling strategy, in which the model of the economy includes as effects of the SMP only those which are explicitly modelled. The model presented in Chapter 5, like the econometric model of Chapter 4, includes both direct effects and competition effects, but excludes any dynamic effects. The model is more elaborate than that used in the econometric estimates, but makes much less use of empirical data, which are used only to calibrate the model numerically, not to test it. To put it crudely, the econometric model is constructed in a way that takes account of theory but is essentially driven by the empirical data, while the CGE model takes account of empirical data but is essentially driven by the theory.

Our research strategy is based therefore on two quite different approaches which have a common analytical underpinning and use data from the same sources. Because they are based on such different methodologies, we should not expect them to give the same answers, but the extent to which their answers diverge will give us some sense of the extent of our true understanding of the nature of the SMP.

2.5. A statistical approach to measuring the trade effects of the internal market

The first research method is based on descriptive statistics of trade performance indicators, and may be described quite briefly. At the two-digit sectoral level we study coverage ratios, the ratios of exports to imports in both intra-EU and extra-EU trade for individual EU countries; and we also undertake market share analysis (or import penetration analysis) at the same sectoral level for the EU as a whole, describing how demand for the products of a sector is divided between domestic products, imports from other EU countries, and imports from non-EU countries.

One problem we have to confront in the statistical analysis is that there was a major SMP-induced change in 1993 in the system of collection of intra-EU trade statistics. Market share analysis provides clear evidence that this change has had quite a strong effect on the statistics. It is unfortunate that the programme whose real effects on trade we wish to analyse had a major impact on the statistics that should be used to identify these effects! In particular, analysis based on coverage ratios is vulnerable to the fact that the statistical impact of the measurement change is likely to be different for exports than for imports; and intra-EU import penetration statistics also have to be interpreted with care. However, making what seems a reasonable allowance for the likely scale of measurement error introduced still leaves considerable evidence of systematic changes in the patterns of intra-EU and extra-EU trade resulting from the SMP.

2.6. Econometric methodology

The use of econometric analysis allows us to separate out the effects of the SMP on trade flows from the impact of other factors such as changes in exchange rates or relative cyclical positions. The analysis is therefore substantially more robust than the crude analysis of descriptive statistics. Our econometric analysis is able to examine the effects of the SMP on both supply and demand within particular markets. In order to derive general equilibrium impact on the European economy as a whole however, we have used a computable general equilibrium (CGE) model, discussed in the next section.

In order to maximize the efficiency of our statistical estimation we have chosen to concentrate the econometric analysis on examining 15 relatively narrowly defined three-digit level industrial sectors. Despite this narrow focus, the sectors taken together account for 35.7% of total EU manufacturing value added. The sectors for analysis were chosen as being the group of larger industries identified ex-ante by Buigues, Ilzkovitz and Lebrun [1990] as likely to be particularly sensitive to the SMP. In addition, we have performed a similar analysis for the manufacturing sector as a whole in order to examine the effect of the SMP on other sectors.

Our econometric analysis has three components:

(a)   First, we follow traditional analyses of trade creation and diversion by examining the direct impact of the SMP on the demand for domestic goods relative to imports from EU and non-EU countries.

(b)   Second, we additionally examine the impact of the SMP on increasing competition between firms and reducing price-cost margins. We model these effects by estimating a set of sectoral price equations.

(c)   Finally, we use simulation techniques to assess the overall impact of the SMP on trade creation and diversion, taking into account both demand and competition factors.

2.6.1. Demand analysis

In the first part of our study we have followed the methodology of traditional econometric studies of trade creation and diversion in accounting for single market effects within the framework of a demand system for imports and domestic goods. The method has been used extensively to examine the effects on trade creation and diversion of the UK's accession to the European Union (Winters [1984]), and recently for a similar study of Spain's accession (Martínez *et al.* [1995]). Previous work on the single market in this tradition includes the work of Brenton and Winters [1992].

The analysis works by estimating the effects of the SMP from adding dummy variables to a set of well specified demand equations, explaining sectoral demand for domestically produced goods and imports from EU and non-EU sources. The demand equations include relative price and overall market demand effects, and hence take into account the impact of changes in exchange rates and relative cyclical positions. The dummy variables therefore only pick up innovations in the pattern of demands, and it is these which we have attributed to the SMP.

The dummy variables have a theoretical identification in terms of SMP effects. The SMP is designed to work both through reducing direct transportation and administrative costs and through the harmonization of standards to increase market access. Intuitively therefore the SMP can be thought of as reducing either the actual or shadow prices of imported goods relative to their price in the exporting country. The latter is measured by using the industry-specific domestic price index in the exporting country.

In our empirical work, we have distinguished between intra- and extra-EU imports. To the extent that reduction in internal EU costs has been achieved by the SMP, we would expect EU exporters' trade shares to have increased and trade perhaps to have been diverted from extra-EU competitors. To the extent that harmonization effects have opened markets to all importers however, both EU and extra-EU imports may have increased.

The 'almost ideal demand' system of Deaton and Muellbauer [1980] is used to model demand for domestic goods and the two sorts of imports. This demand system has been widely used in import demand studies and allows the constraints of consumer demand theory to be relatively easily imposed on the set of estimated equations. The system is particularly well suited to analysis of market shares. The system for domestic consumption, intra-EU imports, and extra-EU imports can be written in the following form:

$$s_d = a_d + g_{dd} \ln p^d / p^r + g_{de} \ln p^e / p^r + b_d \ln Y / P + smd_d$$

$$s_e = a_e + g_{ed} \ln p^d / p^r + g_{ee} \ln p^e / p^r + b_e \ln Y / P + smd_e$$

$$s_r = a_r + g_{rd} \ln p^d / p^r + g_{re} \ln p^e / p^r + b_r \ln Y / P + smd_r$$

The equations explain the shares of total nominal sectoral expenditure (Y) taken by domestically produced goods (s_d), intra-EU imports (s_e) and extra-EU imports (s_r) respectively. The explanatory variables include relative prices and total real sectoral expenditure (Y divided by the aggregate sectoral price index P). The domestic price variable (p^d) is the domestic sectoral producer price index. The prices of intra-EU and extra-EU imports (p^e and p^r respectively) are measured by Paasche indices of individual exporter country sector-specific domestic producer price indices, weighted using 1990 country market shares. The terms a_i, g_{ij}, and b_i are estimated parameters, which can be suitably restricted to conform to the laws of consumer demands. The restrictions are discussed in detail in the Technical Appendix (see A.2.1.1) and include the requirement that the shares add up to unity and that the compensated price responses satisfy Slutsky negativity.

The impact of the SMP is measured through the dummy variables smd_i which can be broadly seen as shifting the constant terms in the equations. If the SMP has been trade-creating, we would expect to find the coefficient of this variable with a negative sign in the domestic market share equation and with a positive sign in the intra-EU import share equation. The sign of the coefficient in the extra-EU import share equation may be either positive or negative, depending on whether the trade creation features of the SMP outweigh its trade diversion effects. Note that the exact identification of these parameters is in fact more complicated and involves the demand parameters: see the derivation in the Technical Appendix (A.2.1.1).

2.6.2. Measuring effects on competition and prices

Demand studies alone do not allow a full assessment of the potential effects of the single market on supply and in stimulating competition. In the second part of our study, therefore, we have gone beyond previous work in attempting to examine the impact of the SMP on supply performance and domestic prices. It is here that the main impacts of the supply improvements caused by increased competition are to be found. These effects were identified by Smith and Venables [1988] and Emerson et al. [1988] as playing an important role in the overall gains expected from the single market.

Our approach to modelling supply is to examine the determination of domestic prices within an explicit oligopoly setting. Domestic firms compete directly with importing firms in setting their prices. Domestic prices in general therefore will depend on domestic costs, the import competitors' prices, and the size of the domestic firms' market share. In response to an increase in competition, such as that generated by the SMP, domestic firms will be forced to reduce their price-cost margins. Our general approach is close to that adopted by Jacquemin and Sapir [1991].

A structural oligopoly model of price competition in an industry where consumer demands are given by an 'almost ideal demand' system has been developed by Allen [1994]. Allen shows that in this context, market shares themselves affect the elasticity of firm own-price demands. A firm whose market share declines will find itself faced with a more elastic own-price elasticity of demand and hence be forced to narrow its price-cost margin.

Allen shows how the model results in log-linear reaction functions, in which a firm's price is a log-linear combination of its own costs and possibly its competitor's prices, with parameters dependent on its conjectural variations of the responses of competitors to changes in own policies. The firm's price equation also contains a constant term, which can be shown to be increasing in the firm's basic market share.

The resultant domestic price equations can be written in the form:

$$\ln p^d = \mu[\alpha \ln w_d + (1-\alpha)\ln m_d + \delta \ln y_d] + (1-\mu)\ln p^m + cnst_d + smpd_d$$

Domestic prices (p^d) are a weighted average (with parameter μ) of domestic marginal costs (the term in square brackets) and competing importer prices. Domestic firms' marginal costs are derived from a Cobb-Douglas cost function and are themselves a weighted average (with parameter α) of unit labour costs (w_d) and other input prices (m_d). Depending on the extent of returns to scale, marginal costs may also be either an increasing or decreasing function of domestic output (as $\delta >,< 0$). Competing import prices (p^m) are measured by a Paasche index of both EU and non-EU importer country sector-specific domestic producer prices, weighted by 1990 market shares. The constant term in the equation $cnst_d$ represents the price mark-up prior to the SMP.

To measure the SMP effects, we again introduce a dummy variable ($smpd_d$). The variable represents innovations in the behaviour of domestic prices relative to before the introduction of the SMP. To the extent that the SMP has increased competition in domestic markets we would expect this dummy variable to be negative. Of course, this effect may be attenuated and even sometimes reversed to the extent that the SMP improves a particular industry's dominance of the overall European market.

2.6.3. Evaluating the overall impact of the single market

To evaluate the overall impact of the SMP on trade creation and diversion in the European Union we must integrate our analyses of the demand and supply effects. To do this we have performed simulations of our estimated equations.

Conventional measures of the market integration effects consider only the demand effects on trade flows. Such estimates ignore the supply-side effects of the single market which work to reduce domestic price-cost margins by increasing competition. In our analysis we have attempted to measure these effects through estimating a set of domestic price equations. These results tell us for each country and industry how domestic prices have been affected by the SMP.

Ignoring these supply-side effects could seriously bias the estimates of the full impact of the single market measures on trade flows. Given that firms will normally be operating on the elastic part of their demand curves, domestic price reductions will tend to some extent to restore domestic loss of market share. This effect will somewhat counteract the direct trade creation effects of the SMP. On average, the share of EU producers' should be expected to rise at the expense of non-EU producers. The extent to which the rise in EU producers' share is distributed between increased domestic share or EU imports depends on whether the most affected countries are net importers or exporters and on the exact set of trade price elasticities.

To derive the full impact of the SMP on both demand and supply, we therefore simulate our set of estimated demand equations, using the domestic price series for home and EU competitor countries adjusted for the dummies estimated in the price equations. The results will give us the additional impact of the supply-side effects on trade flows.

We will thus be able to derive for each country and product category estimates of the full effects of the single market measures on home consumption and intra- and extra-EU trade flows. The full effects can also be decomposed into the impact of the conventionally estimated import price effects on demand and also the additional supply-side effects of increased competitiveness.

2.7. Computable general equilibrium methodology

The objective of the CGE work is to use a fully specified general equilibrium model of trade and production, calibrated to a given year's data set, to investigate the effect on trade flows of the single market programme. We calibrate the model to 1991 data, and the model is then used to project the effect of the single market programme.

The CGE model operates at the same three-digit level as the econometric model, but with more comprehensive sectoral coverage than the econometric model, and it too models producers as imperfectly competitive firms operating in markets with differentiated products. As a fully specified general equilibrium model of trade and production, the CGE model is more elaborate than the econometric model, allowing a richer set of linkages between markets (notably linkages between sectors through the labour markets), but whereas the parameters of the econometric model are estimated on the basis of data series spanning several years, the parameters of the CGE model are imposed, some on the basis of estimates from the literature, and the rest so that the numerical solution of the model reproduces the data of the single base year of 1991.

2.7.1. The model

The details of the model are outlined in Technical Appendix A.2, and more detail is given in Gasiorek, Smith and Venables [1992], who use the same basic model, at a more aggregated level. The underlying theoretical model, just like our econometric model, is based on imperfect competition and increasing returns to scale.

The model has 12 countries: each of the EU countries (with Belgium-Luxembourg treated as a single country) plus the rest of the world. Each country is endowed with three primary factors of production: capital, and manual and non-manual labour. Capital is assumed to be perfectly mobile internationally, and available at a constant price. Other factors are internationally immobile, so their prices adjust to equate demands to endowments. The commodity structure is defined by NACE three-digit industries with the rest of each economy aggregated into a single perfectly competitive composite, which is tradeable and which we take as the *numéraire*. Each of the manufacturing industries is assumed to be imperfectly competitive, with a number of firms producing differentiated products, production being subject to increasing returns to scale.

Demand for differentiated products is modelled as a two-stage process, where the demand for a product aggregate depends on a price index for that aggregate, while demand for an individual variety depends on the price of the variety relative to that of the product aggregate.

We assume that firms act as quantity competitors in segmented markets. Each firm chooses sales in each country market, taking as constant the sales of all its rivals in each market. Optimization requires the equation of marginal revenue to marginal cost in each market, where the slope of each firm's perceived demand curve depends on the extent of product differentiation, and on the share of the firm in that market. The key feature of the model, shared with the theoretical treatment underlying the econometric model, is that price-cost margins thus depend on firms' market shares, and increased import penetration causes firms to behave more competitively, lowering their price-cost margins.

2.7.2. Model calibration and data sources

Numerical calibration of the model and data sources are described in Chapter 5, where the results of the model simulations are reported. The numerical specification of the CGE model is undertaken by first setting some key parameters, notably those describing demand elasticities and returns to scale on the basis of literature estimates, and then calculating the values of remaining parameters and endogenous variables so that the base year observations support an equilibrium.

Trade data were obtained from the COMEXT databank, and the production data primarily from the VISA database. Data on concentration, firm numbers and returns to scale are obtained from the study carried out by Davies and Lyons [1996] and from the survey by Pratten [1988]. In a model based on imperfect competition, data on concentration are crucial, and compared with the work done by Gasiorek, Smith and Venables [1992], the availability of concentration data from the recent work of the Davies and Lyons team, collected on an EU-wide basis and in a way that is more satisfactory than national census data, should considerably improve the reliability of the model. For each sector, Davies and Lyons report a Herfindahl-equivalent number of firms in a Herfindahl-typical EU country, and it is the market share implied by this statistic which we have entered into our imperfectly competitive pricing equations in describing market concentration in the base equilibrium.

It is unusual for general equilibrium modelling to be undertaken at such a disaggregated level, and the reason for working at this level should be made clear. It is not the general equilibrium nature of the analysis that is important. There are general equilibrium effects operating in the model through labour markets, but since the policy changes modelled impact on all sectors in ways that are likely to be unrelated to their factor input characteristics, there is no reason to expect general equilibrium effects to be particularly strong, and the simulations tend to confirm this.

Rather the main motivation for the general equilibrium approach is to have a systematic and consistent treatment of a multi-sector economy. The three-digit level of aggregation is chosen because this seems to be the most appropriate level at which to model interactions between trade policy and market behaviour, and indeed it is the level of aggregation at which we obtain measures of concentration from Davies and Lyons.

2.7.3. Model simulation

One exercise undertaken with the CGE model is an ex-ante simulation, where estimates made in 1990 of the likely effects of the SMP on intra-EU trade costs were imposed on the model and the effects on the equilibrium recomputed. The second kind of exercise undertaken are ex-post simulations, where the values of the changes in trade costs are chosen so as to reproduce as an equilibrium the changes in import penetration observed between 1988 and 1994, on the assumption that producers have, during this time, made only limited adjustments to the change, and the long-run effects of the SMP are then modelled by supposing that there will be subsequent inter-sectoral readjustments in the labour markets and that entry and exit of producers will take place. Two types of ex-post simulation are undertaken, one in which only intra-EU trade barriers are changed, the other in which extra-EU trade barriers are changed in step with intra-EU barriers.

All three simulation exercises are conducted on two alternative assumptions about producer behaviour: the segmented markets hypothesis that firms can set prices independently in each national market of the EU, and the integrated markets hypothesis in which the SMP is supposed to lead firms to start treating the whole EU as a single market.

3. Coverage ratios and competitiveness

The principal objective of this chapter is to examine a range of trade performance indicators in order to search for prima facie evidence of whether the single market programme has affected competitiveness and hence trade flows both within the EU-12 and between the EU-12 and the rest of the world. We focus on two types of descriptive statistics. First, following Buiges, Ilzkovitz and Lebrun [1990], we examine the change in coverage ratios (ratios of exports to imports) over time. This is done for each of the EU-12 countries, for both intra- and extra trade. Secondly, and building on the discussion in Chapter 2, we look at changes in sectoral shares in apparent consumption. For the EU-12 in aggregate, we present changes in shares of home, rest of EU-12, and rest of world producers. All of the descriptive statistical analysis is conducted at the NACE two-digit level. Before the presentation of the descriptive analysis, the first section discusses some of the methodological and empirical difficulties associated with the use of such statistics.

3.1. Methodological and empirical background

At the outset, we need to clarify our interpretation of the controversial concept of 'competitiveness'. Interest in competitiveness reflects concern with how successfully an economy is performing, and a belief that performance relative to other economies provides a natural point of comparison. However, Krugman [1996] has criticized the term as making inappropriate analogies between competition between firms and competition between countries (see also Martínez [1996]). Krugman's key point is that it is the underlying efficiency or productivity of the economy that is the determinant of real income, not performance in foreign markets *per se*.

Performance in foreign markets is influenced by the efficiency of the home economy, but may also be influenced, for example, by wages, exchange rates, and growth rates both in the domestic economy and in partner countries. 'Competitiveness', in the sense of trade performance, should therefore be seen as an imperfect indicator of true economic performance. Thus, when we look in this study at how the SMP may have affected European competitiveness and European trade patterns, the statistics we examine should not be seen as definitive measures but rather as indicators of the possible influence of the SMP.

The trade performance indicators which we consider need to be interpreted with care in the light of changes in macroeconomic variables. We cannot within the scope of a study such as this attempt to take full and formal account of macroeconomic influences on trade patterns, but informal analysis of possible macroeconomic effects is an essential background to the detailed discussion, with exchange rates and growth rates likely to be the significant variables. The unpublished Appendix to this chapter presents data on exchange rates and growth rates for the EU-12 and for the OECD, and this is discussed in more detail below. Our focus is on the effects of the single market, not the effects of exchange rates, but we need to give some consideration to the latter effects if we are going to isolate the former.

3.1.1. Effects of the exchange rate and growth rates

A study by the European Commission [1995] of the exchange rate effects on trade within the single market distinguished between two groups of countries: Group A countries, which have participated in the exchange rate mechanism (ERM) since its inception and among whom bilateral nominal exchange rates have been largely stable; and Group B countries, which have experienced changes, largely devaluations or depreciations, in their nominal and real effective exchange rates. The Group A countries are the Benelux countries, Denmark, Germany, France and Ireland; the Group B countries are Italy, the UK, Spain and Portugal. Changes in exchange rates for the period 1988-94 are detailed in the unpublished Appendix to this chapter. For all the Group A countries the ECU exchange rates remain stable, while the Group B countries see significant depreciations/devaluations in their ECU exchange rates. Patterns in dollar and yen exchange rates are also fairly clear. Following the currency fluctuations earlier in the 1980s, the dollar remained fairly stable throughout this period, while the yen appreciated. Consequently, the Group A countries experienced a fairly stable exchange rate with respect to the dollar, and depreciations with respect to the yen, while the Group B countries experienced depreciations with respect to both the dollar and the yen.

Changes in exchange rates will not necessarily translate into changes in imports and exports. As discussed in the European Commission study, changes in nominal rates may or may not result in changes in real exchange rates, depending on what happens to relative inflation rates, while even changes in real exchange rates may or may not reflect changes in fundamental equilibrium exchange rates: the real exchange rates of a country may be rising because it is becoming more efficient, in which case the direction of causation is from competitiveness to the exchange rate rather than the other way round. There is also the issue of exchange rate pass-through: the more competitive a market is, the more likely it is that home currency prices will react fully to changes in the exchange rate, while imperfectly competitive firms may choose to absorb some of the exchange rate effect on prices in an attempt to maintain market share.

Nevertheless, exchange rate changes will almost surely have some impact upon trade flows, and given what has happened to exchange rates, it would be reasonable to expect that the Group B countries might have increased their competitiveness relative both to the Group A countries, and to the rest of the world, although the extent of these changes would depend on the extent of changes in real exchange rates. Secondly, the changes in the yen relative to all currencies suggests that EU exports to Japan should have become more competitive, while the pattern of change of the US dollar relative to European currencies implies that the exchange rate is less likely to have impacted on competitiveness for Group A countries, but might have for Group B countries.

The unpublished Appendix to this chapter also details the changes in growth rates for the EU (again divided between Group A and Group B countries), the US, Japan, and the rest of the OECD. In all the EU countries except Italy and in Japan, growth rates declined in the period from the late 1980s to 1994. The US and the rest of the OECD witnessed a decline until 1991 and increasing growth rates from 1991 onwards. GDP growth was higher in the EU from 1987 to 1991 than in the US and the rest of the OECD, but fell below the latter's levels in 1992. Growth in the US economy in particular is likely to have increased extra-EU exports, while the decline in growth rates within the EU is likely to have decreased demand for imports.

Against this somewhat confusing macroeconomic background, it is perhaps not surprising that the Commission study finds a diversity of trade performances. So far as costs are concerned, it finds (European Commission [1995], Graph 10, p. 22) – taking the whole period since 1987 and considering real effective exchange rates relative to all trading partners – that of the Group A countries, Germany, Denmark and the BLEU lost cost competitiveness between 1987 and between 1987 and 1994, particularly since 1992, while the gains made by France and the Netherlands before 1992 were not subsequently wholly lost, and Ireland made substantial gains. Among the Group B countries, Italy has significantly improved in cost competitiveness, Greece and Spain lost competitiveness in 1987-90 with some subsequent recovery, Portugal lost competitiveness up to 1992 and then stabilized, and the UK in 1992 regained earlier losses. In intra-EU trade, the gainers in net exports are the BLEU, Denmark, Spain, Ireland, Italy, the Netherlands, and the UK, with Germany and Greece the clearest losers. Changes in extra-EU trade are less clear, but over the period 1987-94 the gainers, measured by extra-EU coverage ratios in volume, were Denmark and Ireland in Group A, while all the Group B countries showed declines in extra-EU trade performance between 1987 and 1992, with recoveries after 1992, Greece and Spain being the countries where the recovery overtook the decline, while the UK's recovery fell far short of the earlier decline.

3.1.2. The INTRASTAT problem

Finally, it is important to note the significant change in the reporting of trade flows within the EU. The adoption of the INTRASTAT system at the start of 1993 has affected the statistics which we use. With intra-EU trade flows reported by companies rather than recorded by customs officials, it is generally believed that there is systematic under-recording of intra-EU trade. Two relevant effects can be identified: under-reporting of 1992 trade flows which were subsequently reported in 1993 (a switch in the allocation of the reporting of trade flows across years); and a generalized under-reporting of intra-EU trade flows following the adoption of the new system. Clearly, the former effect would only have a short-term impact and the use of data up to 1994 should overcome this. With respect to the second effect, there is no reason *a priori* to suppose that it would affect the coverage ratios as they deal with intra- and extra-EU trade flows separately; however, this may well affect the shares in apparent consumption as is discussed in more detail below. (It is also believed that the INTRASTAT reporting system underestimates imports more than exports, since exporters have a greater incentive to report trade flows arising from VAT compensation. For this reason in our analysis we have consistently used export data to measure both intra-EU exports and imports rather than a combination of both export and import data.)

Work in this area done by the UK Central Statistical Office (Williamson and Porter [1994]) suggests that the situation is complex. Adjustments made to initial estimates of imports in 1993 are worth about 1% of overall EU imports. In addition, the data prior to 1992 have been adjusted downwards by some 3.5%, due to imports from the rest of the world through Rotterdam being improperly classified as EU imports. Unfortunately, the CSO were not able to allocate such trade on an industrial level. The total net effect of the UK CSO adjustments would appear to be to change the relative balance of EU and non-EU imports between 1992 and 1993 by some 8% of total EU imports. The UK figures might be an extreme case.

3.2. Coverage ratios

We now turn to look for evidence that the single market programme has had effects on the pattern of sectoral competitiveness both within the EU and in extra-EU markets, whether by giving more scope for traditional comparative advantage to influence trade patterns or by encouraging competitive restructuring.

Our first set of descriptive statistics are coverage ratios, which have the advantage of incorporating information about the destination of production as well as the origin of consumption. The intra-EU coverage ratio is the ratio of exports to imports in a given industry in intra-EU trade, while the extra-EU coverage ratio provides the same calculation for extra-EU trade. Note that, statistical errors aside, the average intra-EU coverage ratio within each sector should be 1, since intra-EU exports are equal to intra-EU imports.

The intra-EU coverage ratio should reflect how the SMP (and other economic changes in the period) have affected the pattern of competitiveness within the EU, whether by giving more scope for traditional comparative advantage to influence trade patterns or by encouraging competitive restructuring. Extra-EU coverage ratios should indicate how the SMP (and other economic changes) have changed market shares of non-EU producers in EU markets and the competitiveness of EU producers in non-EU markets.

Table 3.1.   **Direction of change in coverage ratios, 1988-94: Group A countries**

NACE	IRL Intra	IRL Extra	D Intra	D Extra	F Intra	F Extra	B/L Intra	B/L Extra	NL Intra	NL Extra	DK Intra	DK Extra
21	⇓	⇓	⇑	⇑	⇑	⇓	⇓	⇑	⇓	⇓	⇑	⇔
22	⇔	⇑	⇑	⇓	⇑	⇓	⇑	⇑	⇑	⇑	⇓	⇓
23	⇑	⇑	⇑	⇑	⇔	⇑	⇑	⇓	⇓	⇑	⇑	⇓
24	⇑	⇓	⇑	⇔	⇑	⇓	⇑	⇔	⇔	⇔	⇓	⇓
25	⇑	⇑	⇑	⇑	⇑	⇑	⇔	⇔	⇑	⇓	⇑	⇓
26	⇑	⇑	⇑	⇑	⇑	⇔	⇑	⇑	⇓	⇓	⇑	⇓
31	⇑	⇓	⇑	⇓	⇑	⇓	⇑	⇔	⇑	⇔	⇓	⇓
32	⇑	⇔	⇑	⇑	⇑	⇑	⇔	⇓	⇑	⇑	⇔	⇓
33	⇔	⇑	⇔	⇑	⇑	⇓	⇓	⇑	⇑	⇑	⇔	⇑
34	⇔	⇔	⇑	⇑	⇑	⇑	⇑	⇔	⇑	⇑	⇑	⇔
35	⇓	⇓	⇑	⇑	⇔	⇔	⇑	⇔	⇑	⇓	⇓	⇑
36	⇔	⇔	⇓	⇑	⇔	⇑	⇓	⇓	⇓	⇑	⇓	⇑
37	⇓	⇑	⇑	⇑	⇑	⇔	⇑	⇑	⇔	⇑	⇓	⇑
41	⇔	⇔	⇓	⇑	⇑	⇑	⇑	⇑	⇔	⇑	⇑	⇓
43	⇑	⇓	⇑	⇓	⇑	⇔	⇑	⇓	⇑	⇔	⇑	⇑
44	⇑	⇓	⇑	⇑	⇔	⇑	⇑	⇔	⇔	⇔	⇔	⇑
45	⇑	⇓	⇑	⇓	⇔	⇔	⇑	⇔	⇔	⇓	⇔	⇓
46	⇑	⇓	⇑	⇔	⇑	⇑	⇑	⇔	⇑	⇑	⇑	⇓
47	⇔	⇑	⇓	⇔	⇑	⇑	⇑	⇑	⇑	⇔	⇔	⇑
48	⇑	⇓	⇑	⇔	⇔	⇓	⇑	⇓	⇔	⇑	⇔	⇓
49	⇑	⇑	⇔	⇔	⇔	⇓	⇓	⇓	⇓	⇓	⇓	⇓
91	⇑	⇑	⇑	⇑	⇑	⇔	⇑	⇔	⇑	⇑	⇑	⇔

Table 3.2.   Direction of changes in coverage ratios 1988-94: Group B countries

NACE	UK Intra	UK Extra	I Intra	I Extra	E Intra	E Extra	P Intra	P Extra	GR Intra	GR Extra
21	⇓	⇑	⇑	⇓	⇑	⇑	⇓	⇓	⇑	⇓
22	⇑	⇓	⇔	⇓	⇓	⇑	⇑	⇓	⇔	⇓
23	⇑	⇑	⇑	⇑	⇓	⇑	⇑	⇑	⇓	⇓
24	⇓	⇔	⇑	⇓	⇔	⇑	⇑	⇑	⇔	⇑
25	⇔	⇑	⇓	⇓	⇔	⇓	⇔	⇑	⇔	⇓
26	⇔	⇔	⇓	⇓	⇔	⇑	⇑	⇓	⇑	⇓
31	⇓	⇓	⇑	⇓	⇑	⇓	⇓	⇓	⇑	⇓
32	⇓	⇔	⇑	⇓	⇑	⇑	⇑	⇑	⇑	⇑
33	⇓	⇔	⇑	⇓	⇓	⇓	⇓	⇑	⇑	⇓
34	⇓	⇓	⇑	⇑	⇑	⇑	⇑	⇑	⇑	⇑
35	⇓	⇑	⇓	⇑	⇔	⇑	⇑	⇔	⇑	⇔
36	⇓	⇑	⇔	⇓	⇔	⇓	⇑	⇑	⇑	⇑
37	⇓	⇓	⇑	⇔	⇑	⇔	⇑	⇑	⇑	⇑
41	⇓	⇑	⇑	⇓	⇓	⇔	⇓	⇔	⇑	⇔
43	⇑	⇑	⇑	⇓	⇔	⇓	⇓	⇓	⇓	⇓
44	⇑	⇔	⇑	⇔	⇓	⇑	⇔	⇔	⇓	⇑
45	⇔	⇓	⇑	⇓	⇔	⇓	⇓	⇓	⇓	⇓
46	⇓	⇓	⇑	⇔	⇓	⇓	⇔	⇑	⇑	⇓
47	⇔	⇑	⇔	⇔	⇓	⇓	⇓	⇓	⇑	⇓
48	⇓	⇔	⇑	⇔	⇑	⇓	⇔	⇓	⇑	⇑
49	⇓	⇑	⇑	⇔	⇔	⇓	⇓	⇑	⇓	⇓
91	⇓	⇓	⇓	⇔	⇔	⇔	⇔	⇑	⇑	⇓

We have calculated the intra-EU and extra-EU coverage ratios for each country, for each two-digit industry from 1980 to 1994. Even at the two-digit level, this is a formidable volume of statistics, and it proved difficult to draw any clear messages from it. The unpublished Appendix to this chapter shows the changes in sectoral coverage ratios and for manufacturing as a whole (NACE 91) for France; and Tables 3.1 and 3.2 summarize the change in the coverage ratios over the period 1988-94 for each country and industry. Table 3.1 shows the changes in coverage ratios for the Group A countries and Table 3.2 for the Group B countries. The comparison period 1988-94 was chosen in order to be able to span a period including both pre-SMP and post-SMP years.

The change for NACE 91 (all manufactures) should give some indication of the macroeconomic influences discussed in the previous section. The patterns shown do not correspond completely to those shown in the Commission study. The modest rise in the intra-EU coverage ratio in all countries must be a purely statistical phenomenon, probably reflecting changes in the reporting of intra-EU imports and exports. Certainly, there is little evidence that the countries which depreciated in 1992 gained much competitive advantage with respect to EU partners.

Over the period 1988-94 the seven Group A countries all experienced a rise in their overall intra-EU coverage ratios, while of the Group B countries, only one experienced a rise, two a fall, and two little change. This suggests increasing competitiveness for the Group A countries and decreasing competitiveness for the Group B countries. The depreciations in 1992 do not seem to have given the latter group much competitive advantage with respect to EU partners, though the exchange rate changes do seem to have arrested a longer term decline in their overall coverage ratios. These overall effects can also be seen by summarizing the effects across all the industries as in Table 3.1. For the Group A countries the intra-EU coverage ratio rose in 80 cases, declined in 22 and remained more or less stable in 29. For the Group B countries, the corresponding figures are 50, 37 and 22.

It is perhaps with respect to extra-EU coverage ratios that one has to be particularly careful about influences contemporary with, but independent of, the SMP, especially macroeconomic variables; and indeed the pattern of changes in extra-EU coverage ratios is more mixed. Over the period 1988-94 the extra-EU ratio for manufacturing as a whole for the Group A countries rose in three cases and fell in three, while for the Group B countries there was only one increase in the ratio, a decline in two cases and little change in two cases. Except for Greece, the early 1990s again appear to show an arresting of a more long-term decline in the aggregate coverage ratio for the Group B countries. It might be tempting again to attribute this to the effect of the exchange rate changes outlined earlier. However, the similar pattern for the Group A countries seems to indicate that there were other factors affecting the coverage ratios.

A count of the different changes shown in Tables 3.1 and 3.2 again suggests differences between the two groups of countries. For the Group A countries an increase in the extra-EU coverage ratio occurred in 54 cases, a decline in 43 and little change occurred in 34 cases. For the Group B countries the corresponding figures are 39, 49 and 21. Declines in the extra-EU coverage ratios thus occurred more frequently for the Group B countries than for the Group A countries. This seems to indicate that changes in competitiveness are at least not dominated by exchange rate effects, and that extra-EU macroeconomic influences are not strong enough to wipe out intra-EU differences between countries.

We turn now to inter-industry differences and to attempt to find a 'story', we look more closely at two countries, France and Spain, the former of which seems at the aggregate level to be gaining in competitiveness in the period, the latter not. As we discussed above, the coverage ratios we present will also have been affected by changes in the underlying macroeconomic conditions. However, there is no strong reason to suppose a priori that these macroeconomic effects should have a differential impact on industries within a country. For example, an exchange rate depreciation should, all things being equal, increase the coverage ratios in all sectors. By examining individual countries and looking across industries, we can to some extent filter out macroeconomic effects.

Turning first to France, and to manufacturing industry in aggregate, both the intra-EU and the extra-EU coverage ratios show a rise in the period from 1991 onwards, with the greater rise being that in the intra-EU ratio, and with a small dip in the extra-EU ratio in 1993/94. There are several factors worth noting here. First, as discussed above, the total manufacturing intra-EU coverage ratio for the whole of the EU tends to rise, and this must be some kind of statistical artefact (since we have used export data for all intra-EU trade flows in order to reduce the INTRASTAT problem). Secondly, the higher growth rates in the rest of the OECD would tend to increase the extra-EU coverage ratios. Thirdly, the depreciation of the franc with respect to both the dollar and the yen is also likely to increase the extra-EU coverage ratio. While it is interesting, therefore, that the change in the intra-EU coverage ratio is more positive, it is hard to argue that there is convincing evidence of strong effects from the SMP.

It is more interesting therefore to look at changes in the coverage ratios at a more disaggregated sectoral level. There are no sectors in which the intra-EU coverage ratio declines, there are 14 sectors in which it rises, and 6 in which it is more or less stable. For those industries which experience a rise in the intra-EU coverage ratio, this rise appears to reflect a change from the pattern in the 1980s for NACE 21, 26, 31, and 44. The extra-EU coverage ratio shows much more variation. It declines in 7 industries, rises in 9, and is stable in 4. Of the industries which experience a rise, this appears to reflect a change in the previous pattern for NACE 25, 32, 34, 36, 41 and 47. Finally, in 6 of the sectors which experience a rise in the extra-EU coverage ratio, this is also accompanied by an increase in the intra-EU coverage ratio.

The message of these statistics is mixed. Nevertheless, it does seem that for France, (i) the changes in external competitiveness have been more varied across sectors than the changes in internal competitiveness, (ii) the changes in internal competitiveness appear to be greater than those in external competitiveness, and (iii) despite an aggregate increase in both coverage ratios, there remains considerable sectoral variation, which suggests that although there were macroeconomic factors affecting competitiveness, they were not sufficient to eliminate microeconomic differences between sectors.

Comparing France and Spain, we see considerable sectoral variation in both countries, with no particular similarities between the corresponding columns for the two countries, or the two columns for either country. Indeed, looking across the columns at all the countries in both tables, we see the same message emerge. At this level of commodity aggregation, therefore, it seems difficult to argue that there is positive evidence of a link between changes in intra-EU competitiveness and in extra-EU competitiveness, or of strong common forces affecting sectoral competitiveness in both countries. Nevertheless, despite the variation, it is clear that the number of cases in which the coverage ratios increase is greater than the reverse, and this is true for both sets of countries; while with respect to the extra-EU coverage ratio it is true only for the Group A countries.

When we look at cross-national patterns in the sectoral changes, there are few sectors in which one might discern a pattern in either the intra- or the extra-EU coverage ratio changes. In NACE 25 it is clear that the Group A countries have largely increased their intra-EU coverage ratios, while the Group B countries have experienced a decline. There are other sectors where similar patterns might be discerned, but in a less marked way. These include NACE 24, NACE 26, NACE 43 and NACE 46. In NACE 31 and NACE 32 both the Group A and the Group B countries appear to experience an increase in the intra-EU ratio (though this must be the statistical anomaly referred to already). With regard to extra-EU coverage ratios there appears to be a loss in competitiveness for both sets of countries in NACE 31, NACE 43, NACE 45, and NACE 48. Given the nature of these sectors, the loss of competitiveness since 1990 is to be seen as the continuation of a longer-run trend rather that a break with past performance induced by the SMP. There is some increase in competitiveness in NACE 22, NACE 34, NACE 36, and NACE 37. NACE 34 (electrical engineering) is a sector in which the SMP might be expected to have strong effects, and there does indeed seem to be a break with past performance in many countries. For the remaining industries, the picture is more mixed.

3.3. Shares in apparent consumption

The second type of data we present are changes in shares in apparent consumption. Apparent consumption is equal to total domestic consumption from domestic or foreign sources; and here we present the shares from home sources (Home), imports from the EU (EC) and imports from the rest of the world (RoW). Consumption shares should be less volatile than coverage ratios and less affected by macroeconomic differences between countries, although undoubtedly exchange rate effects may be present.

The last set of graphs in the unpublished Appendix to this chapter details the consumption shares at the NACE two-digit level for the EU-12 in aggregate. Rather than presenting simply a comparison of consumption shares in a pre-SMP period with a post-SMP period, the graphs show the evolution of the shares over time, and hence can help shed light on whether any changes in the shares from the early 1990s onwards are part of a more long-term trend, or might be attributable to the SMP.

It must be noted, however, that the interpretation of consumption shares is vulnerable to the statistical problems that arise from the change in the methods of recording intra-EU trade from 1993 onwards, discussed in Section 3.1.2 above. Arising from our earlier discussion of CSO estimates of the scale of the INTRASTAT problem, we also show in the charts what the shares would be if the figure for intra-EU trade were increased by 10% in 1993 and 1994. In some sectors, notably NACE 22, 24, 25, 26, 34 and 43A, this 10% adjustment does seem to iron out anomalies in the pattern of share changes over time. There are other sectors, however, such as 23, 31 and 32, where a counter-intuitive fall in the EU share remains even after the adjustment. On the basis of the adjusted shares, it does appear that in most industries there has been an increase in the EU share over the period in question. In some cases this change in share is very modest (NACE 22, 34, 35, 43A and 48); in some there does appear to be a decline (NACE 23, 32, 45 and 46); while in others the rise is significant (NACE 26, 33, 36 and 37).

Fortunately, the impact of the adjustment on RoW shares is in most sectors very slight, so that recorded changes in these shares, on which we focus as the prime measure of the possible impact of the SMP on external competitiveness, might be taken as reasonably robust to measurement errors. These changes in the rest of the world share could, of course, be driven by exchange rate changes, or by changes in the underlying competitiveness of the rest of the world producers.

The charts show that in most sectors, EU markets have become increasingly open to imports from the RoW, with changes in the 1990s being the continuation of a longer-run trend. The chemicals sector (NACE 25) is a clear example, in which the intra-EU import share has risen steadily too, and motor vehicles (35), food, drink and tobacco (41) show the same changes, with man-made fibres (26) only a little less regular in the pattern of change over time. Metal manufactures (31), mechanical engineering (32), textiles (43A), and paper (47) show an increasing pace of RoW import penetration, even allowing for the possibility that intra-EU trade is understated in these cases even after the 10% adjustment. Office machinery (33), other transport (36), and instrument engineering (37) all show a speeding up in the 1990s of the decline in home market shares, with the clear suggestion that the SMP or other changes in the 1990s have increased the openness of markets to imports from the RoW as well as the EU. There is some, but less strong, indication of an increase in the trend to openness in 34 (electrical engineering) also.

Figure 3.1.   Import penetration ratios, all manufacturing, EU total, 1980-94

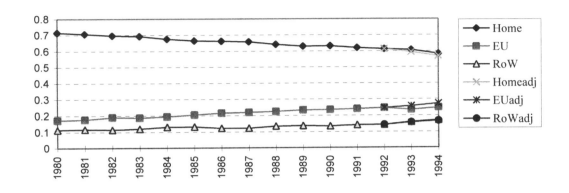

A summary chart for aggregate manufacturing for all EU countries is presented as Figure 3.1 and shows how the 10% adjustment in intra-EU imports is sufficient to put this share back on trend, but is not enough to slow the decline of the share of home producers or the rise in the share of extra-EU imports. The message that the SMP seems to have opened EU markets to non-EU producers rather than closing them off seems fairly robust to the possible measurement errors associated with INTRASTAT.

Given the pattern of changes in these graphs, and given the discussion of exchange rates earlier, it does not appear likely that exchange rate changes are driving these results. Where the rest of the world share has increased in all cases, this is not represented by a significant change in the late 1980s and early 1990s, but appears to be part of a longer-term trend. This would suggest that it is taking place as a result of the increasing openness of the world trading system, which is serving to reduce the domestic market shares at the expense of both rest of the world and EU producers. In this context it is worth noting that the increasing intra-European openness arising from the SMP might also have increased the attractiveness of the European market for rest of the world producers, and for similar reasons.

3.4. Conclusion

Given the multiplicity of influences on trade balances and the theoretical slipperiness of the idea of competitiveness, it is perhaps unsurprising that investigation of coverage ratios at the two-digit level has thrown up several interesting observations, but has failed to provide unambiguous evidence of the effects of the SMP on trade patterns. The analysis is best taken as providing indications that the issue is worth pursuing in a more systematic fashion.

By contrast, changes over time in consumption shares seem to be less vulnerable to short-term macroeconomic influences and to display patterns that are more informative as a result. There are clearly too many different factors to be taken into account for an approach based on descriptive statistics to make further progress, and we now turn to more systematic and disaggregated methods of analysing the different forces at work, with consumption shares being the focus of our analysis.

4. An econometric evaluation of the single market programme: data, estimation, and results

This chapter presents the results of an econometric examination of the impact of the single market programme (SMP) on trade flows and price competition in the EU. The use of econometric analysis allows us to separate out the effects of the SMP on trade flows and price competition from the impact of other factors such as changes in exchange rates or relative cyclical positions. The analysis enables us to examine the effects of the SMP on both demand and supply within particular industrial markets.

The structure of the chapter is as follows. The first section presents the scope of our study and the data sources used (Section 4.1). The econometric analysis is then presented in the next three sections. The analysis has three components:

(a) Firstly, we follow traditional analyses of trade creation and diversion in examining the direct impact of the SMP on the demand for domestic goods relative to imports from EU and non-EU countries (Section 4.2).

(b) Secondly, we also examine the impact of the SMP on increasing competition between firms and reducing price-cost margins. We model these effects by estimating a set of sectoral price equations (Section 4.3).

(c) Thirdly, we use simulation techniques to assess the overall impact of the SMP on trade creation and diversion, taking into account both demand and competition factors (Section 4.4).

Section 4.5 discusses our results in detail at the industry level. Finally, Section 4.6 contains our overall conclusions.

4.1. Data sources and the scope of the study

Our analysis has concentrated on behaviour in the four major EU economies – Germany, France, Italy, and the UK – principally for data availability reasons. The tables in the unpublished Appendix to this chapter, however, contain estimation results for a wider range of countries for particular industries.

For each country and industry pair, we have distinguished between three sources of supply to domestic markets: home production, imports from other EU countries, and imports from non-EU suppliers. For the purposes of this study, the EU is defined as the 12 states which were members in 1992, so excluding Sweden, Finland, and Austria.

The primary data source used in this study is the Eurostat VISA industrial database, supplemented by data from the OECD and the International Monetary Fund (IMF). The Eurostat VISA database is dated September 1995. It contains annual data on a three-digit NACE industry level for the original European 12 countries plus the USA and Japan. For the principal four EU countries, Germany, France, Italy, and the UK, data are in most cases available for the period 1976-94. Data are available for other EU countries on a more restricted basis, generally for the period 1980-94. The data for the most recent period, 1993 and 1994, are preliminary and have been estimated by Eurostat statisticians using the results of industry-level surveys.

In order to restrict the size of our investigation and to maximize the efficiency of estimation, we have used narrowly defined three-digit NACE industry data for 15 manufacturing sectors which account for 35.7% of total EU manufacturing value-added. These sectors were chosen as being the group of larger industries identified ex-ante by Buigues, Ilzkovitz and Lebrun [1990] (subsequently referred to as BIL [1990]) as being particularly sensitive to the SMP. Additionally, we have performed a similar analysis for manufacturing industry as a whole in order to be able to examine the effects of the SMP on other manufacturing sectors.

The study therefore presents estimated impacts of the SMP on the following 15 sensitive sectors:

247	Glassware
248	Ceramics
251	Basic industrial chemicals
257	Pharmaceutical products
315	Boilermaking etc.
322	Machine tools for metals
324	Machine tools for foodstuffs
325	Plants for mines
330	Office machines
344	Telecommunications equipment
345	Electronic equipment
351	Motor vehicles
364	Aerospace equipment
427	Brewing and malting
453	Clothing

In addition we have presented aggregate results for manufacturing industry as a whole, for the 15 sensitive sectors aggregated together, and for the rest of manufacturing industry.

4.1.1. Market shares

Sectoral information on current price gross domestic production, exports, and imports from EU and non-EU sources is available directly from the VISA database. The data are in current prices valued in ECU. To derive a measure of the overall domestic market size for the products of a particular sector from these data, we have derived a measure of total sectoral domestic market size or 'apparent domestic consumption' defined as gross domestic production (variable 68) minus total exports (variable 200) plus intra-EU imports (variable 110) and extra-EU imports (variable 111). The share of domestic goods in the overall market is then defined as domestic production minus exports divided by total market size. Intra-EU and extra-EU import shares are analogously defined.

4.1.2. Domestic prices

Our study has used sectoral domestic price indices. These have been derived from the VISA database and are the implicit price deflator of gross output defined as current price gross domestic production (variable 68) divided by gross domestic production valued at 1990 constant prices (variable 868). In some cases, the latter variable is not available prior to 1980 for France, Italy, and some of the smaller countries. In this instance, we have used an aggregate domestic producer price series to interpolate the industry price data back to 1976 in order to derive a full price series matrix. Details of the series used are given in the unpublished Appendix to this chapter.

4.1.3. Import prices

Sectoral import price data disaggregated by source of goods are not available. In order to derive import price series for intra-EU and extra-EU imports we have made use of competitor sectoral domestic price indices. Overall price indices for intra-EU and extra-EU import competitors have been derived from the original country data using a Paasche index of sectoral competitor domestic prices. The intra-EU indices use a set of sectoral competitor prices for the other 10 EU countries (Belgium and Luxembourg are combined in the data), weighted according to 1990 sectoral import value shares. The extra-EU indices are based on sectoral domestic prices for the US and Japan, given the weights respectively of non-Japanese and Japanese import shares in total 1990 non-EU imports.

4.1.4. Unit labour costs and producer input prices

In order to estimate our price equations we need measures of manufacturing input costs. These have been derived from IMF and OECD sources. We have used aggregate manufacturing cost measures in order to reduce simultaneity problems. Unit labour cost data have been obtained from the IMF, and measures normalized unit labour costs in manufacturing in local currencies. The measures are widely used to derive international cost competitiveness measures. Two measures of input materials costs have been used, each derived from OECD Main Economic Indicators data. The sectoral level equations use a measure of overall manufacturing producer prices. The latter is clearly required, since we are modelling gross output prices and intermediate goods from other sectors of manufacturing. For the aggregate manufacturing price equations we have used a measure of import prices. As a measure of real output to capture cyclical effects, we have used gross output at 1990 prices (VISA variable 868).

4.2. Econometric demand analysis of the effects of the single market programme

4.2.1. Estimation methodology

We first present the results of a traditional demand-based analysis of trade creation and diversion as a result of the SMP. As is explained in Section 2.6, we consider this to provide only a partial assessment of the full impact of the SMP, which needs to be augmented by a study of supply-side effects (discussed in the next section). The demand-side method uses dummy variables to assess the effects of the SMP from a set of well specified demand equations. The demand equations include relative price and overall market demand effects, and hence take into account the impact of changes in exchange rates and relative cyclical positions. The dummy variables therefore only pick up innovations in the pattern of demands, and it is these which we have attributed to the SMP. The method has been used extensively to examine trade creation and diversion effects of trade liberalization (see Winters [1984], Martínez *et al.* [1995], [1996], and Brenton and Winters [1992]).

For each of the four principal countries, Germany, France, Italy, and the UK, and for a number of the smaller countries, we have estimated demand equations at the three-digit NACE industry level. We distinguish between three sources of supply to domestic markets: home production, imports from other EU countries, and imports from outside the EU.

In our estimation of the demand equations we are faced with very small sample sizes. We typically have just 18 observations from 1976 to 1994 on the four largest countries (Germany, France, Italy, and the UK) and 14 observations from 1980 to 1994 for some of the other countries. In the circumstances it is important to obtain the most parsimonious and efficient possible estimates.

We have used the 'almost ideal demand' system of Deaton and Muellbauer [1980] to model sectoral demand for domestic goods, intra-EU imports and extra-EU imports. To preserve degrees of freedom, we have estimated a partial adjustment system with a diagonalized adjustment matrix. The requirements of consumer theory, homogeneity and symmetry, were imposed to ensure the efficiency of the estimates. Time trends were initially excluded from the estimates. This was the maximal feasible estimating system given the constraints of the small sample of data. Our system of equations can be written in the following form:

$$\Delta s_{ht} = i_{ss}.(a_h + g_{hh}.\ln p_t^h / p_t^r + g_{he}.\ln p_t^e / p_t^r + b_{hy}.\ln Y_t / P_t - s_{ht-1}) + smd_d$$

$$\Delta s_{et} = i_{ss}.(a_e + g_{he}.\ln p_t^h / p_t^r + g_{ee}.\ln p_t^e / p_t^r + b_{ey}.\ln Y_t / P_t - s_{et-1}) + smd_e$$

$$\Delta s_{rt} = i_{ss}.(a_r + g_{hr} \ln p_t^h / p_t^r + g_{re}.\ln p_t^e / p_t^r + b_{ry}.\ln Y_t / P_t - s_{rt-1}) + smd_r$$

The equations explain the shares of total nominal sectoral expenditure (Y) taken by domestically produced goods (s_h), intra-EU imports (s_e) and extra-EU imports (s_r) respectively. The explanatory variables include relative prices and total real sectoral expenditure (Y divided by the aggregate sectoral price index, P). The domestic price variable (p^h) is the domestic sectoral producer price index. The prices of intra-EU and extra-EU imports (p^e and p^r respectively) are measured by Paasche indices of individual exporter country sector-specific domestic producer price indices, weighted using 1990 country market shares.

The parameter i_{ss} is the partial adjustment coefficient which is common to all equations in order to ensure adding up. The terms a_i, g_{ij}, and b_i are the parameters of the long-run consumption share equations and have been suitably restricted to conform to the laws of consumer demands. The restrictions are discussed in detail in the Technical Appendix to this chapter and include the requirement that the shares add up to unity and that the compensated price responses satisfy Slutsky negativity.

The impact of the SMP is measured through the dummy variables smd_i which can be broadly seen as shifting the constant terms in the equations. If the SMP has been trade-creating, we would expect to find the coefficient of this variable with a negative sign in the domestic market share equation and with a positive sign in the intra-EU import share equation. The sign of the coefficient in the extra-EU import share equation may be either positive or negative, depending on whether the trade creation features of the SMP outweigh its trade diversion effects.

SMP dummy variables have been added for each of the years from 1992 to the end of the sample period, 1994. We have then calculated their sum weighted by the adjustment coefficient to obtain their permanent effect. The period from 1992 onwards is considered to be the period during which most of the SMP legislation was actually activated. Where substantial SMP effects were seen prior to 1992, this should be revealed by our extensive model misspecification testing.

For the empirical estimation of this system we have used maximum likelihood to estimate the full set of parameters simultaneously. A full covariance matrix was estimated, since we have relatively low dimensionality and to avoid possible misspecification. The specification of our models was extensively tested. Full details of estimation techniques and test statistics are contained in the Technical Appendix to this chapter.

We first ensured that our models were validly conditioned in order to make further statistical inference possible. The specification was extensively tested for autocorrelation, autoregressive heteroscedasticity (ARCH), and non-normality. The results of the tests are reported in the unpublished Appendix tables. Dynamic respecification and/or additional dummy variables (and in a small number of cases time trends) have been entered into the equations as a result of these tests. There was no evidence of higher than first-order empirical dynamics.

To ensure the conformity of our equations with consumer demand theory, we have tested for conformity with Slutsky negativity. Where necessary, this has been imposed on our estimates. Details of the method used are contained in the Technical Appendix. The unpublished Appendix tables report when negativity has been imposed, together with the set of eigenvalues of the substitution matrix in the 1990 base year. The set of own-price uncompensated or Marshallian elasticities is also reported.

4.2.2. Results

Table 4.1 summarizes our econometric estimates of the direct effects of the single market on market shares in our different industrial sectors. The full econometric results for the estimated demand equations are presented in Tables A.4.D1 to D16 in the unpublished Appendix. The sectoral impacts of the SMP on relative demands are derived from the calculation of the permanent effect of the sets of SMP dummy variables included in the set of well-specified demand equations.

There is considerable evidence that the direct demand impact of the SMP has been to reduce domestic producer market shares. The demand-side effects of the SMP are estimated to have reduced domestic market shares by 2.2% in manufacturing as a whole and on average by 5.4% in our 15 sensitive sectors. A negative demand-side effect on domestic market shares is found in every sector studied.

The estimated SMP demand impacts on domestic producer shares in general are larger than the actual changes in market share which have been experienced. This is strong evidence that the supply-side effects of the SMP cannot be ignored. Increased competition has substantially reduced domestic price-cost margins and improved domestic competitiveness (see Section 4.3). Thus actual domestic market shares have actually been more buoyant than the impacts suggested by the SMP demand-side effects alone.

Table 4.1.   Estimated direct demand impact of single market programme by sector

	% change in market share			Share of total import change	
	Home	EU	RoW	Intra-EU imports	RoW imports
247 Glassware	-1.3	-0.1	+1.4	-0.08	1.08
248 Ceramics	-4.2	+1.8	+2.4	0.43	0.57
251 Basic industrial chemicals	-4.3	+2.5	+1.8	0.58	0.42
257 Pharmaceuticals	-1.9	+0.4	+1.5	0.21	0.79
315 Boilermaking etc.	-5.3	+4.4	+0.9	0.83	0.17
322 Machine tools for metals	-2.0	-2.2	+4.2	-1.10	2.10
324 Machine tools for foodstuffs	-7.4	+3.0	+4.4	0.41	0.59
325 Plant for mines	-1.7	+1.0	+0.7	0.59	0.41
330 Office machines	-7.8	+2.8	+5.0	0.36	0.64
344 Telecommunications equipment	-2.7	+1.7	+1.0	0.63	0.37
345 Electronic equipment	-15.7	+4.6	+11.1	0.29	0.71
351 Motor vehicles	-4.9	+3.7	+1.2	0.76	0.24
364 Aerospace equipment	-15.3	+14.6	+0.8	0.95	0.05
427 Brewing and malting	-6.3	+5.9	+0.4	0.94	0.06
453 Clothing	-2.9	-2.5	+5.4	-0.86	1.86
Weighted average for 15 sensitive sectors	-5.4	+3.0	+2.5	0.55	0.46
Rest of manufacturing	-0.4	-0.9	+1.3	-1.60	2.60
Aggregate manufacturing	-2.2	+0.5	+1.7	0.23	0.77

Note: Estimated direct demand effect of SMP is calculated as the average of the estimates for Germany, France, Italy and the UK.

There is no evidence of any substantial effect of the demand-side effects of the SMP reducing the market share of extra-EU imports. On the contrary, the direct impact of the SMP is estimated to have increased extra-EU imports by 1.7% in manufacturing as a whole and by 2.5% in our 15 sensitive sectors.

The estimated impact of the SMP on intra-EU trade may be affected by the under-recording of trade flows between EU states. Even so, the demand-side effects of the SMP are estimated to have increased intra-EU trade shares by 0.5% in manufacturing as a whole and by 3% in the

15 sensitive sectors. The apparent contraction in intra-EU imports in the imputed rest of manufacturing sector, however, may be evidence that intra-EU imports have been underestimated owing to the introduction of the INTRASTAT system at the beginning of 1993, as discussed in Section 3.1.2 above. Were intra-EU imports in the rest of manufacturing in fact to have increased by the same proportion as extra-EU imports in that sector, then intra-EU imports as a whole may have been underestimated on average by 1-2% of overall market size (5-10% of overall intra-EU imports). If this is the case, the demand impact of the SMP on intra-EU imports in the 15 most sensitive sectors may in fact have been substantially larger than the estimated 3%.

Despite possible under-recording, the estimated numbers for our 15 sensitive sectors suggest that EU importers have gained slightly more market share than non-EU importers in these industries. This pattern is repeated throughout the industries studied. In every industry the estimated demand effect of the SMP on the domestic market is negative. The average impact on import shares of both EU and non-EU producers is positive in all but two industries.

Examining the estimated direct demand effects on intra- versus extra-EU imports allows us, despite possible underestimation, to make some assessment of the extent to which the SMP measures themselves were multilateral rather than just intra-EU in their effects. Figure 4.1 shows comparison of the relative estimated demand impacts of the SMP on the market shares of EU and non-EU producers respectively. Amongst the industries experiencing the largest impacts, two different groups can be distinguished.

Figure 4.1.   Changes in trade partner market shares

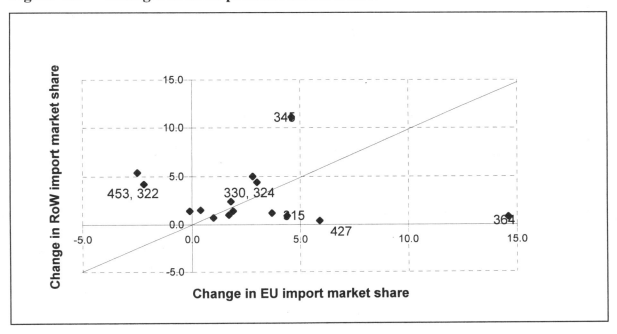

First, there are a number of industries in which there has been a major estimated positive impact on EU import share with very little impact on non-EU producers. This is most clear in the aerospace industry (NACE 364), but the phenomena can also be seen in brewing (427), boilermaking (315), and motor vehicles (351). These might be seen as the industries in which the SMP has benefited EU trade most.

In contrast, in a second set of industries there is evidence that the SMP has multilaterally improved trade access. In these sectors, the estimated gains of non-EU producers outweigh and sometimes are estimated to have reduced EU importer shares. Particularly large relative impacts are found in electronic equipment (NACE 345), office machines (330) and machines for foodstuffs (324). Large gains in rest of the world (RoW) producer shares, accompanied by actual falls in the EU import share have been experienced in the clothing (453) and machine tools for metals (322) industries.

4.3. Econometric estimates of the effects of the single market programme on price competition

4.3.1. Estimation methodology

Demand studies alone do not allow a full assessment of the potential effects of the SMP on supply and in stimulating competition. In the second part of our econometric study, we have therefore gone beyond previous work in examining the impact of the SMP on supply performance and domestic prices. It is here that the main impacts of the supply improvements caused by increased competition are to be found. These were identified by Smith and Venables [1988] and Emerson *et al.* [1988] as playing an important role in the overall gains expected from the single market.

In order to assess the effects of the SMP on price competition, we have therefore estimated a second set of equations for sectoral domestic prices in each country. The equations are based on an explicit oligopoly model as explained in detail in Chapter 2 (Section 2.6.2). Domestic firms compete directly with importers in setting prices. Therefore, in general, domestic prices will depend on domestic costs, import competitors' prices, and the size of the domestic firms' market share. In response to an increase in competition such as that generated by the SMP, domestic firms will be forced to reduce their price-cost margins.

Our estimated equations take the following form:

$$\Delta \ln p_t^d = \lambda . \{ \mu \ [\alpha \ln w_{dt} + (1-\alpha) \ln m_{dt} + \delta \ln(y_{dt}) + \pi] + (1-\mu) . \ln p_t^m + cnst_d - \ln p_{t-1}^d \} + semp_{dt}$$

To preserve degrees of freedom and improve efficiency of estimation we have adopted a simple partial adjustment formulation of the price equations with price homogeneity imposed. The log change in domestic prices (p_t^d) depends on the difference between the firms' optimal prices and their previous period's actual prices. Optimal prices are a weighted average (with parameter μ) of domestic marginal costs (the terms in square brackets) and competing importer prices. Domestic marginal costs are themselves a weighted average of domestic unit labour costs (w_{dt}) and other input prices (m_{dt}). Marginal costs also depend on the scale of output (y_{dt}) and technical progress (denoted by the time trend t). Competing import prices (p_t^m) are measured by a Paasche index of both EU and non-EU importer country domestic producer prices weighted by 1990 import shares. The constant term ($cnst_d$) represents the price mark-up prior to the introduction of the SMP.

To measure the SMP effects, we have introduced a set of dummy variables into the estimated equation ($semp_{dt}$). These variables represent innovations in the behaviour of domestic prices relative to before the introduction of the SMP. To the extent that the SMP has increased competition in domestic markets, we would expect these variables to be negative. Of course, this effect may be attenuated or even reversed to the extent that the SMP improves a particular industry's dominance of the European market.

SMP dummy variables have been again added for each of the years from 1992 to the end of the sample period, 1994. We have then calculated their sum weighted by the adjustment coefficient to obtain their permanent effect. The period from 1992 onwards is considered to be the period during which most of the SMP legislation was actually activated. Where substantial SMP effects were seen prior to 1992, this should be revealed by our extensive model misspecification testing.

Table 4.2. **Estimated price competition impact of the single market programme on price-cost margins**

	% change
247 Glassware	-4.0
248 Ceramics	-3.0
251 Basic industrial chemicals	-6.2
257 Pharmaceuticals	-7.0
315 Boilermaking etc.	-4.8
322 Machine tools for metals	-6.7
324 Machine tools for foodstuffs	-1.4
325 Plant for mines	-4.3
330 Office machines	-15.7
344 Telecommunications equipment	-4.6
345 Electronic equipment	-1.1
351 Motor vehicles	+2.2
364 Aerospace equipment	-6.6
427 Brewing and malting	-0.1
453 Clothing	-1.8
Weighted average for 15 sensitive sectors	-3.9
Rest of manufacturing	-3.4
Aggregate manufacturing	-3.6

In estimating these price equations, we have again been faced with very small sample sizes of 18 or 14 years. We have therefore employed the most efficient and parsimonious estimation techniques. For our final estimates, we have used iterative non-linear SURE to estimate the set of different country equations for each sector simultaneously. The specification has been extensively tested for autocorrelation, autoregressive conditional heteroscedasticity (ARCH), and non-normality. The equations have been dynamically respecified and/or additional dummy variables have been entered into the equations as a result of these tests. Full details of the estimation techniques and test statistics are contained in the Technical Appendix to this chapter.

4.3.2. Results

Summaries of our estimates of the SMP effect on price-cost margins are presented in Table 4.2. The full set of estimated equations are presented in Tables A.4.P1 to P16 in the unpublished Appendix. Our estimates of the impact of the SMP on price-cost margins are given by the calculated permanent effect of the SMP dummy variables included in the estimated price equations.

The results suggest that the SMP has been successful in stimulating additional price competition. Conditional price-cost margins have fallen in total manufacturing by 3.6% since 1991, and by an average of 3.9% in the 15 sensitive sectors. This phenomenon is experienced widely throughout the set of industries examined. In all but motor vehicles (351) the average industrial conditional price-cost margin has contracted since the introduction of the SMP.

To examine the movements in price-cost margins further, it is interesting to consider possible reasons for differences in their behaviour between industries. As often emphasized in the pre-implementation literature (see Emerson *et al.* [1988] and Winters [1994]) the impact of the SMP will affect industries in different ways depending on the exact nature of the single market measures implemented and their interaction with the nature of competition within a particular industry.

Average sectoral movements in price-cost margins are plotted against changes in conditional domestic market shares in Figure 4.2. In those industries suffering the largest shocks (over 5% to either prices or market shares), we can distinguish two very different sorts of reaction.

Figure 4.2.   Changes in price-cost margins and domestic market shares

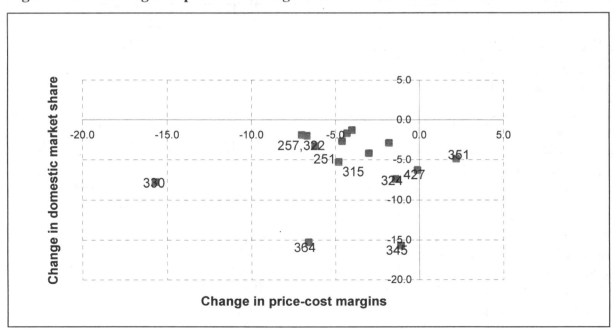

In the first group, there are large falls in price-cost margins accompanied by relatively small changes in market share. This group is composed of office machines (NACE 330), pharmaceutical products (NACE 257), machine tools for metals (322) and basic industrial chemicals (251). These industries appear to have chosen to reduce prices rather than lose market share.

In the second group, large falls in market share are accompanied with only small falls in price-cost margins. This group consists of electronic equipment (NACE 345), machine tools for foodstuffs (324), brewing and malting (427), and perhaps the aerospace equipment industry (364).

All these industries are relatively oligopolistic as measured by concentration ratios (see Table 5.1 in the next chapter). Clearly, market structure and conduct differ between the two groups, although there is no evidence in the data available to us of systematic differences in concentration or in returns to scale between the two groups. One could conjecture that those firms in the first group of industries prefer to reduce prices to keep market share, perhaps because of the existence of switching costs (not implausible in any of the three sectors). These costs may be less significant in the second group of industries where fixed mark-ups may maximize profits, despite a consequent loss of market share.

These results differ considerably from the behaviour we would expect in a competitive industry with diminishing returns to scale. Then we would expect an increase in external competition to be reflected both in reductions in price margins and market shares. Interestingly, the behaviour of the boilermaking (NACE 315) and clothing (453) industries, two of the most competitive in the sample as measured by concentration ratios, show large reductions in both price margins and market shares.

4.4.   Assessing the overall impact of the single market programme on trade flows: the *Antimonde*

4.4.1. Simulation methodology

To examine the overall impact of the single market on trade flows, we need to ask what the outcome in the absence of the set of policies would have been. Effectively we must derive an *Antimonde* (or alternative world). To do this, we need to take account of both the estimated direct effects on trade flows and the further impact on trade flows of the estimated reductions in price-cost margins within EU countries.

The direct effects of the single market on trade flows represent the result of the reduction in the actual costs of trade (for instance, from the simplification of administrative procedures) and reductions in shadow costs (as a result of technical harmonization). Theoretically, these should result in a fall in domestic market share, a rise in EU market share, and have an indeterminate effect on non-EU producers. We have discussed in detail the empirical results for these effects in the last section.

To obtain the full effects of the single market policies, however, we need also to consider the impact of increased competitiveness on trade flows. The theoretical mechanism here is that the single market measures increase competition in EU domestic markets and reduce price-cost margins. Given that firms will normally be operating on the elastic part of their demand curve, price reductions will tend to increase their overall revenue and, to some extent, restore their loss of market share. The impact of this effect therefore will, to some extent, be to counteract the direct effects of the single market. On average, the share of EU producers should be expected to rise at the expense of non-EU producers. How exactly the rise in EU producers' share is distributed between increased domestic share or EU imports depends on whether the most affected countries are net importers or exporters, and on the exact set of trade price elasticities.

As discussed in the previous section, we have found considerable evidence that domestic price-cost margins have fallen substantially and statistically significantly in nearly all the industries studied. It is therefore important to examine the additional impact of competitiveness effects on trade flows.

We have simulated these competitiveness effects using our estimated results for both demand and price equations. Our estimates of the reduction in price-cost margins as a result of the single market are given by the dummy variables in our price equations. For the four major economies (Germany, France, Italy, and the UK) we have then simulated the impact of the price reductions on trade flows using our estimated demand equations.

Because of the limited amount of information on the smaller economies, we have had to extrapolate the change in EU importers' prices by using information on the major economies. The change in domestic prices is given by the domestic price-cost margin dummy; the change in overall EU prices, however, has been proxied by taking the average of the price-cost dummies in the other three main EU countries.

4.4.2. Evaluating the effects of competition on market shares

Summaries of the results of our simulations of the overall estimated impact of the SMP are given in Tables 4.3 and 4.4. Table 4.3 decomposes the overall estimated impact of the SMP on market shares into direct demand-side effects and the effects of increased price competition. Table 4.4 compares our overall estimated effects with the actual changes in market shares over the period 1991-94. Full details of the individual country and industry simulations are given in the unpublished Appendix Tables A4.S1 to A4.S16.

The simulation results demonstrate that it is essential to consider the supply-side effects of the SMP on increasing competition to obtain a full evaluation of the programme. The results suggest that the overall shifts in trade shares are overestimated by the use of the traditional direct effects analysis.

In the 15 most sensitive sectors, taking into account the competition impact tends to lower our estimate of the impact of the SMP on domestic market shares. In the sensitive sectors on average, improved price-cost margins are estimated to have restored domestic market shares by 1.2%, roughly a quarter of our estimate of the reduction caused by direct demand effects. This occurs in all but two of the sectors.

The estimated competition effect in the same industries on EU importer shares is generally negative. This seems to be the result of the fact that the competition effects on prices occur mainly in previously protected net importer markets. The major net exporter countries appear to experience less change in their price-cost margins. This may be either because the single market has less effect on their domestic markets than with the net importing countries, or because some of the domestic market loss may be offset by higher exports. Non-EU importer shares are reduced by the competition effects as expected.

Table 4.3.   Overall estimated impact of the single market programme by sector

| | % change in market shares | | | | | | | | |
| | Direct demand | | | Price competition | | | Overall impact | | |
	Home	EU	RoW	Home	EU	RoW	Home	EU	RoW
247 Glassware	-1.3	-0.1	+1.4	+0.7	-0.1	-0.5	-0.7	-0.2	+0.9
248 Ceramics	-4.2	+1.8	+2.4	-0.2	+0.3	-0.1	-4.4	+2.0	+2.4
251 Basic industrial chemicals	-4.3	+2.5	+1.8	+1.1	-0.7	-0.3	-3.3	+1.8	+1.5
257 Pharmaceuticals	-1.9	+0.4	+1.5	-0.1	+0.2	-0.1	-2.0	+0.5	+1.4
315 Boilermaking etc.	-5.3	+4.4	+0.9	+0.9	-0.9	+0.0	-4.4	+3.5	+0.9
322 Machine tools for metals	-2.0	-2.2	+4.2	-0.6	+0.2	+0.4	-2.6	-2.0	+4.6
324 Machine tools for foodstuffs	-7.4	+3.0	+4.4	+0.5	-0.4	-0.1	-6.9	+2.6	+4.3
325 Plant for mines	-1.7	+1.0	+0.7	+1.1	-0.6	-0.5	-0.6	+0.4	+0.2
330 Office machines	-7.8	+2.8	+5.0	+1.1	+0.1	-1.2	-6.7	+3.0	+3.8
344 Telecommunications equipment	-2.7	+1.7	+1.0	+1.0	-1.5	+0.5	-1.7	+0.2	+1.5
345 Electronic equipment	-15.7	+4.6	+11.1	+4.0	-2.2	-1.8	-11.7	+2.2	+9.5
351 Motor vehicles	-4.9	+3.7	+1.2	+0.3	-0.7	+0.3	-4.6	+3.0	+1.5
364 Aerospace equipment	-15.3	+14.6	+0.8	+7.0	-2.5	-4.4	-8.3	+12.0	-3.8
427 Brewing and malting	-6.3	+5.9	+0.4	+1.5	-1.4	-0.1	-4.8	+4.5	+0.3
453 Clothing	-2.9	-2.5	+5.4	+0.7	-0.5	-0.2	-2.1	-3.1	+5.2
Weighted average for 15 sensitive sectors	-5.4	+3.0	+2.5	+1.2	-0.8	-0.4	-4.2	+2.1	+2.0
Rest of manufacturing	-0.4	-0.9	+1.3	-0.8	+0.4	+0.4	-1.2	-0.4	+1.7
Aggregate manufacturing	-2.2	+0.5	+1.7	-0.1	+0.0	+0.1	-2.3	+0.5	+1.8

The results seem more ambiguous for manufacturing as a whole. Despite a general lowering of price-cost margins, only small price competition effects are found on market shares. This principally reflects the lower demand price elasticities found in our estimates of the demand equations for manufacturing as a whole. To the extent that this is a result of aggregation issues, the competition effects may be underestimated for the manufacturing sector as a whole.

Our estimates of the overall impact of the SMP taking into account both demand and competition effects, suggest that it has been strongly trade creating. The overall impact on domestic market shares is estimated to have been 4.2% in the 15 sensitive sectors and 2.3% in manufacturing as a whole.

Table 4.4.   Comparison of the overall estimated impact of the SMP with actual 1991-94 changes

| | % change in market shares | | | | | |
| | Estimated overall impact | | | Actual changes | | |
	Home	EU	RoW	Home	EU	RoW
247 Glassware	-0.7	-0.2	+0.9	-1.6	+0.3	+1.3
248 Ceramics	-4.4	+2.0	+2.4	-2.8	+0.8	+2.0
251 Basic industrial chemicals	-3.3	+1.8	+1.5	-1.5	-0.0	+1.5
257 Pharmaceuticals	-2.0	+0.5	+1.4	-3.7	+1.6	+2.1
315 Boilermaking etc.	-4.4	+3.5	+0.9	-1.2	+0.9	+0.3
322 Machine tools for metals	-2.6	-2.0	+4.6	+0.3	-5.4	+5.1
324 Machine tools for foodstuffs	-6.9	+2.6	+4.3	-0.9	-1.7	+2.6
325 Plant for mines	-0.6	+0.4	+0.2	-0.9	-0.7	+1.6
330 Office machines	-6.7	+3.0	+3.8	-9.2	+4.0	+5.2
344 Telecommunications equipment	-1.7	+0.2	+1.5	-1.3	+0.2	+1.2
345 Electronic equipment	-11.7	+2.2	+9.5	-15.2	+5.6	+9.6
351 Motor vehicles	-4.6	+3.0	+1.5	-1.8	+0.2	+1.5
364 Aerospace equipment	-8.3	+12.0	-3.8	-11.6	+8.2	+3.4
427 Brewing and malting	-4.8	+4.5	+0.3	-2.1	+2.1	+0.0
453 Clothing	-2.1	-3.1	+5.2	-4.9	-1.6	+6.5
Weighted average for 15 sensitive sectors	-4.2	+2.1	+2.0	-3.7	+1.0	+2.7
Rest of manufacturing	-1.2	-0.4	+1.7	-2.3	-0.1	+2.4
Aggregate manufacturing	-2.3	+0.5	+1.8	-2.8	+0.3	+2.5

It is also clear that there is little evidence of trade diversion. The overall impact of the SMP is estimated to have increased extra-EU import shares by 2% in the 15 sensitive sectors and by 1.8% in overall manufacturing.

The extent of the SMP impact on intra-EU trade is affected by the under-recording of trade flows between EU states as a result of the introduction of the INTRASTAT system. Nevertheless, even using the published data, we estimate that the SMP has increased intra-EU imports by 2.1% in the 15 sensitive sectors and by 0.5% in manufacturing as a whole. Almost certainly these effects are considerably underestimated.

4.5.   Discussion of the detailed results by industry

4.5.1.   Glassware (NACE 247)

Glassware is one of the industries that BIL [1990] classify as suffering from moderate non-tariff barriers. Certainly it had one of the highest net price dispersions found amongst industries in the EU.

Overall, our results show a substantial reduction of some 4% in price-cost margins and a moderate 1.3% fall in domestic market shares. The fall in market share was almost entirely picked up by non-EU producers.

On a country level, our results show a divergence in experience. There is a considerable and significant loss of domestic market share in Italy and the UK by 6% and 5% respectively. The market gains are roughly shared amongst EU and non-EU exporters. In contrast, in Germany there is evidence of a significant rise in the domestic share and no change in the French own share.

Our equations for price-cost margins also show differences in country experience. French, Italian and Belgian price-cost margins fall statistically significantly from 5% to 10%. German price-cost margins have narrowed but not significantly, and there is no significant evidence of movements in UK margins.

4.5.2.   Ceramics (NACE 248)

According to BIL [1990], ceramics was an industry with moderate non-tariff barriers but high internal EU price dispersion. Clearly, this is an industry in which the direct reduction in transport costs should have some impact.

Our overall results suggest that the SMP has had a major effect. Price-cost margins have narrowed on average by 3%, whilst average domestic market shares have contracted by 4.2%. The fall in domestic shares has largely been equally shared by increased EU and non-EU import shares.

On a country level, there have been big falls in domestic market share in Italy and the UK. In both countries EU importers have been the major beneficiaries. A smaller, non-statistically-significant fall in domestic share has occurred in Germany, though here non-EU importers have made the major gains. The French domestic share has stood up well, partly replacing EU imports.

The results for price-cost margins show falls in Germany, France and the UK. Italian price-cost margins have slightly widened.

4.5.3.   Basic industrial chemicals (NACE 251)

The basic industrial chemicals industry was moderately concentrated and suffered from moderate non-tariff barriers according to BIL [1990]. Because of data coverage problems results are only available for Germany, France, Italy, and Spain. The lack of data for the UK in this industry is clearly an important omission.

Overall price-cost margins have fallen by a substantial average of 6.2%, whilst average domestic market shares have fallen by 3.3%. This has been shared between EU and non-EU importers in the ratio 3:2.

On a country basis, the results show a loss of domestic market share in France, Italy, and Spain, in each case with substantial gains being made by EU importers. The German domestic market share has expanded at the cost of other EU imports to the German market.

Price-cost margins have declined in all four countries considered. Domestic price-cost margins have fallen by 12% in Italy, 7% in France, and by 2-3% in Germany and Spain.

4.5.4. Pharmaceutical products (NACE 257)

Pharmaceutical products was a sector dominated by highly regulated markets and public procurement. It is a highly concentrated industry with price controls in many countries (see Emerson *et al.* [1988]). The sector appears to have undergone major structural change since 1991.

The results of the demand equations are presented in the unpublished Appendix. All of the equations except for Greece were dynamic. They are reasonably well conditioned, with some evidence of autocorrelation only in France, Denmark, and Portugal, none of which is significant at the 1% level. Dummies were required in 1989 for Greece and 1991 for Belgium, with post EU-entry dummies significant in both Spain and Portugal.

Most of the equations had poorly determined price effects and except in the case of France, Denmark and Ireland price negativity had to be imposed using the WSB technique. This is perhaps not surprising given the nature of an industry dominated by public procurement. Engel curve effects were in general significant and almost universally (except for Portugal and Ireland) classified domestic goods as necessities and foreign (either EU or RoW) goods as luxuries.

Overall, the sector has witnessed some major changes as a result of the SMP. On average, price-cost margins have declined by 7%, whilst domestic market share has fallen by only 1.9%. Both EU and non-EU producers have gained from the loss of domestic market share.

On a country basis, statistically significant falls in home market share have taken place in Italy, Belgium, Spain, and Portugal, with non-significant falls of share in most other countries. More varied are the gainers: in almost all cases, non-EU imports have grown, significantly in Italy, the UK, Belgium, and Portugal. Imports from EU sources have risen in Italy, Belgium, Spain, and Portugal, but fallen in Denmark, Greece and Ireland. These results are not changed by the sensitivity test.

The domestic price equations for this sector have been estimated for Germany, France, Italy, the UK, and Belgium. Competitor prices play a limited role in all equations except in Italy. There is some evidence of economies of scale in production.

There have been substantial falls in price mark-ups since 1991 in all of the countries, ranging from 5% in the UK and Belgium to over 10% in Italy.

4.5.5. Boilermaking, reservoirs, and sheet-metal containers (NACE 315)

The boilermaking etc. industry is characterized by high domestic market shares in the larger countries, Germany, France, Italy, the UK, and Spain.

The equations are well conditioned, except for some residual non-normality in the French and Danish equations. Price effects are well determined in the major economies. Most elasticities are modestly elastic.

Overall, the industry has seen major falls in both price-cost margins and domestic market shares. Average price-cost margins have contracted by 4.8%, whilst domestic market share has fallen by an average 5.3%. Other EU producers have been the main beneficiaries.

Statistically significant home market share losses have taken place in Germany, Italy, the UK, and Spain. In all but Germany, EU importers have been the principal beneficiaries. Non-EU importers have gained in Germany.

The price equations for Germany, France, Italy, the UK, and Belgium have been estimated. Only the UK and Belgian equations contain competitor prices, but these are large and significant in each case.

There is some evidence of substantial narrowing of price margins in France and Italy by 12% to 14%. German price-cost margins appear to have risen slightly. There has been almost no change in price margins in the UK and Belgium.

4.5.6. Machine tools for metals (NACE 322)

The machine tools for metals industry faces moderate non-tariff barriers according to the BIL [1990] study. Prior to the SMP the industry had modest concentration ratios and a high level of both intra- and extra-EU trade.

The industry overall has seen quite large falls in its price-cost margins of 6.7% on average, whilst experiencing only a small average fall in market share of 2%. A major feature of our results, however, has been a switch from EU towards non-EU importers.

The individual country results show falls in market share in German and French markets, largely in favour of non-EU importers. In Italy and the UK, non-EU producers have gained again, but at the expense of EU imports rather than domestic sales.

Price-cost margins have fallen statistically significantly in Germany, France, and Italy from 6% to 13%. Margins have risen in the UK.

4.5.7. Machine tools for foodstuffs (NACE 324)

The machine tools for foodstuffs industry again faced moderate non-tariff barriers. It was relatively modestly concentrated and had a high level of intra- and extra-EU trade prior to the SMP.

Overall, the industry has seen a large reduction in domestic market share by 7.4%, whilst experiencing only a small 1.4% average reduction in price-cost margins. The loss in domestic market share has been shared approximately equally between EU and non-EU producers.

On an individual country basis, domestic producers have seen very substantial losses in domestic market share in France, Italy, and the UK. The Italian loss of 23% was particularly large and was statistically significant. Gains in market share in these countries were shared almost equally between EU and non-EU producers. There appears to be evidence of similar behaviour in the Belgian market, but the dummies here have to be interpreted in the light of some clear discrepancies between the Eurostat estimates of trade and production data.

The situation in Germany contrasts with experience in other countries. German domestic market share increased by 4.3%, particularly at the expense of other EU country importers.

Movements in price-cost margins largely reflect behaviour in market shares. French and Belgian price-cost margins fall statistically significantly by 4%, whilst German margins rise by a similar percentage (although this is not strictly statistically significant).

4.5.8. Plant for mines (NACE 325)

The plant for mines industry faced moderate non-tariff barriers according to the BIL [1990] study. It was moderately concentrated and had a high average trade ratio of EU and non-EU trade of over 50% of domestic markets.

Overall, the industry has suffered moderate falls in price-cost margins by an average 4.3%, whilst also seeing a modest decrease in domestic market shares. The domestic market share loss was approximately shared between EU and non-EU exporters.

Amongst the individual countries, both France and Italy lost domestic market share to a mix of EU and non-EU imports. The Belgian experience seems to be similar, but the interpretation of this is affected by some statistical problems with the extrapolations of Belgian production and trade data. In Germany and the UK, in contrast, domestic market shares rose, in the German case from reduced EU import share, in the UK from reduced non-EU import share.

Statistically significant falls in price-cost margins were experienced in France and Belgium by 13% and 4% respectively, with a non-significant fall in Italy by 3%. German price-cost margins fell by 1%, whilst UK margins remained almost stable.

4.5.9. Office machines (NACE 330)

The office machines industry includes the computing industry. It is characterized by high-technology and a high (25%) but not dominant public sector procurement share (Emerson *et al.* [1988]). The computer industry is characterized by single domestic firms competing against mainly non-EU producers.

The overall results show substantial falls in both price-cost margins by an average 15.7% and domestic market shares by 7.8%. Both EU and non-EU import shares have risen, with the greater gain being by non-EU producers.

All the demand equations are well conditioned and most are dynamic. Dummies were required in 1982 for Italy, 1981 and 1987 for Belgium, and 1984 and post EU-accession for Spain. Only Germany, France and Italy have large domestic market shares with a smaller but significant share (16%) in the UK. This causes difficulty in determining price elasticities, and except for Germany and France, price negativity has been imposed. Domestic income share elasticities are negative in Germany and France, but positive in Italy and Belgium.

There have been some substantial shifts in conditional market shares since 1991. Domestic market shares have declined except in Germany, with dramatic falls in France, Italy, Spain and Ireland. Both EU and non-EU import shares have risen in France, Italy, and the UK. Non-EU producers have gained at the expense of EU importers in Belgium and Ireland, whilst EU producers gained in Spain. Behaviour in the German market is interesting: both domestic and non-EU importers appear to have gained at the expense of EU importers.

Results for price-cost margins are available for Germany, France, Italy, and the UK. In the price equations, competitor prices are important in France and Italy. There is little evidence of scale effects.

Very substantial reductions in price-cost margins have occurred in France, Italy, and the UK. Prices have fallen by from 16% in France and to over 30% in the UK. German price-cost margins have not changed significantly.

4.5.10. Telecommunications equipment (NACE 344)

The market for telecommunications equipment is characterized by large monopsony, usually public-sector, purchasers of equipment, and considerable differences in standards. There was little existing intra-EU trade in this sector, although more with economies outside the EU. Emerson *et al.* [1988] note that there are potentially considerable economies of scale in the market. The SMP has concentrated on opening up public procurement and the harmonization of standards.

The results for the demand equations are only available for the major producers: Germany, France, Italy, the UK, and Spain. Except for the UK, price effects are relatively poorly determined as might be expected in a regulated market. Germany, France, and Italy had negativity imposed using the WSB technique.

There has been a relatively large fall in price-cost margins in the main four countries by an average 4.7%. In contrast, there has been relatively little movement in market shares, with an overall 2.7% fall in domestic market shares shared approximately equally between EU and non-EU producers.

Amongst the individual countries, the only statistically significant evidence of changes in market shares occurs in Spain where the domestic conditional market share has fallen by over 20% of the market, largely to the benefit of other EU producers. Smaller and non-significant falls in market share, again largely to the benefit of other EU producers, occur in France and Italy.

Substantial and significant falls in price-cost margins occur in both France and the UK by 15% and 9% respectively. There is evidence of a rise in price-cost margins in Italy and little change in Germany. Unfortunately, results for Spanish price-cost margins are not available.

4.5.11. Electronic equipment (NACE 345)

Data on the electronic equipment industry are available for the main four economies plus Spain. As part of the SMP, the sector has seen moves towards technical standardization. In general, our demand equations are reasonably well determined as might be expected in a consumer sales industry. Except in Italy, all the equations are dynamic.

The industry has seen a major drop in domestic market share of 5.7%, particularly concentrated in Italy and the UK. Average price-cost margins in contrast have fallen by only 1.1%

Amongst the individual countries, conditional domestic market shares have fallen most in the UK and Italy, by 48% and 10% respectively. Non-EU importers have gained most from the UK decline, whilst both EU and non-EU producers appear to have gained in Italy. Non-statistically-significant reductions in domestic share have occurred in the other countries.

Price-cost margins in the industry have fallen significantly in Germany and France. UK margins have also fallen, whilst Italian margins appear to have actually widened.

4.5.12. Motor vehicles (NACE 351)

The motor vehicle industry appears to have behaved rather differently from other industrial sectors in the EU, perhaps as a result of factors we have not been able to consider, such as the role of non-EU direct investment within the sector. Unfortunately full data sets for the sector are only available for Germany, France, Italy, and Spain. In particular, the lack of data for the UK is a serious omission.

On average, price-cost margins seem to have widened in the industry. This is despite a loss of domestic market share by 4.9%, which, however, is concentrated in Italy and Spain.

From the demand equations we can see a divergence in behaviour between the German and French markets and those in Italy and Spain. German and French domestic market shares have held up, whilst precipitate falls have occurred in Italy and Spain. In each of the latter cases, other EU producers appear to have been the principal gainers.

As might be expected in the light of the demand results, the price equations show a variety of responses in price-cost margins. These results, however, are not clear cut. German price margins have fallen statistically significantly, whilst French margins have remained roughly unchanged. Paradoxically, Italian margins have risen, whilst Spanish margins are unchanged. Presumably, these results reflect the supply behaviour of the multinational firms which dominate this industry.

4.5.13. Aerospace equipment, manufacture and repair (NACE 364)

The aerospace industry is fairly concentrated within the EU with a relatively small number of firms within the EU whose principal competitors are in the rest of the world. Potentially, intra-EU technical harmonization would allow increased exploitation of economies of scale.

Results for the demand equations are available for the four main economies plus Spain. As might be expected in a relatively monopsonistic industry, the price effects in the demand equations were not well determined, and negativity had to be imposed in each case.

Overall, both price-cost margins and domestic market shares have fallen substantially on average by 6.6% and 15.3% respectively. The main gainers have been other EU producers.

On an individual country basis, there have been large falls in domestic market share in France and Spain, largely benefiting other EU producers. German and UK conditional domestic market shares appear to have increased at the expense of non-EU producers.

Price equations are available for the four largest economies only. In France there is evidence of competitors' prices being significant in determining mark-ups. Economies of scale are statistically significant in Germany and France.

Since 1991, price-cost margins appear to have fallen in a statistically significant manner by 15% in France and 7% in Italy, and have also fallen in Germany and the UK.

4.5.14. Brewing and malting (NACE 427)

The brewing and malting industry is characterized by exceptionally high domestic market shares in each of the countries studied, the typical domestic share being over 90% of the market. The industry suffered from a variety of non-tariff barriers and tax discrimination in favour of domestic producers (Emerson *et al.* [1988], pp. 67-71). Full data sets are available for the core five and Spain and Portugal.

Most of the equations are static, with the exception of Italy. This might be expected in a mainly consumer oriented industry. The German equation required the addition of a (negative) time trend. The equations are generally well conditioned. Price effects are reasonably well determined with own price domestic elasticities around unity and larger import price elasticities.

The results show major falls in domestic market share on average by 6.6%, whilst price-cost margins have remained relatively stable. The market share gains have on average largely been by other EU producers.

Since 1991, significant falls in conditional domestic market share have occurred in France (-2.4%), Italy (-24.6%), and Spain (-2.0%), largely to the benefit of other EU importers. The statistics show that domestic suppliers have increased market share marginally in the UK by 0.9%, but these figures are distorted by the non-recording of household sales.

The price equations for the sector show that despite the low foreign market shares, competitor prices are significant in Italy, the UK, and Belgium. There is little evidence of significant price margin reductions, except in Italian prices.

4.5.15. Clothing (NACE 453)

Prior to the single market, the clothing sector was characterized by a relatively high level of integration between EU producers, but the internal frontiers that were needed to distribute Community quotas amongst Member States *vis-à-vis* third-country producers mean that the market was far from integrated (Emerson *et al.* [1988], pp. 79-82). The clothing sector has relatively low import shares relative to textiles.

Full data sets for the clothing industry are only available for Germany, France, Italy, the UK, and Belgium. The equations are static except for Italy. They are well conditioned, except for some mild autocorrelation in the Belgian equations. Price effects are reasonably well determined except for Germany. Own-price elasticities are around unity.

Overall, there is evidence of modest falls in both price-cost margins by 1.8% and domestic market shares by 2.9%. EU producers appear also to have lost market share to non-EU importers.

There is evidence of post-1991 gains in RoW import conditional market share everywhere (though not significant in France) by 2% to 15%. This is at the expense of domestic market shares in Italy and Belgium and EU import shares in Germany and the UK.

The price equations are entirely based on costs. Modest, but statistically significant falls in price margins were experienced in Germany, France, and Italy.

4.6. Overall conclusions

In this chapter we have described the building, estimation and simulation of an econometric model in 15 narrowly defined three-digit NACE manufacturing sectors, to look for SMP effects. The sectors, accounting for 35.7% of total EU manufacturing value added, were identified ex-ante by BIL [1990] as being particularly sensitive to the SMP. Additionally, we have performed a similar analysis for manufacturing industry as a whole in order to be able to examine the effects of the SMP on other manufacturing sectors.

For each country, we have estimated econometric models of both demand and price equations to examine the extent to which recent behaviour in these industries has been significantly different from past experience. By this method we are able to derive residual imputation measures of both the direct effects of the SMP on trade flows, and also the effects of the programme on domestic price-cost margins. Through simulations, we are able to derive the overall impact of increased EU competitiveness on trade flows.

To assess the overall impact of the SMP, we have considered both demand- and supply-side effects of the programme. The direct demand-side effects come from the reduction in the cost of importing. These may facilitate only intra-EU imports or potentially both intra- and extra-EU imports together. In addition, however, we have considered the supply-side effects of the SMP in increasing price competition in domestic markets. These effects were identified by Smith and Venables [1988] and Emerson *et al.* [1988] as playing an important role in the overall gains expected from the single market.

The direct impact of the single market on demand has been trade creating, both for EU and non-EU producers. There is little evidence of any substantial trade diversion of non-EU trade. As shown in the summary Table 4.5, the direct demand impact of the SMP is estimated to have reduced domestic market shares by 5.4% on average in the 15 sensitive sectors, and by 2.2% in manufacturing as a whole. EU and RoW producers are estimated to have both gained from the SMP, roughly in the same proportion. A similar pattern is repeated throughout the industries studied.

The single market measures have also been found to have improved price competition and reduced price-cost margins. Our estimated price equations are conditioned on a linearly homogeneous combination of domestic costs and competitor prices. They also take into account cyclical effects through the term in output. Despite this, we estimate that the SMP has compressed price-cost margins by 3.9% on average in the 15 sensitive sectors and by 3.6% in manufacturing as a whole. This behaviour is reflected generally amongst industries. In all but one industry the industrial average conditional price-cost margin contracted.

Table 4.5.   Summary of estimated impacts of the SMP and actual changes, 1991-94

(%)

	Average 15 sensitive sectors			Rest of manufacturing			Total manufacturing		
	Home	EU	RoW	Home	EU	RoW	Home	EU	RoW
Estimated demand impact of SMP	-5.4	+3.0	+2.5	-0.4	-0.9	+1.3	-2.2	+0.5	+1.7
Estimated competition impact of SMP	+1.2	-0.8	-0.4	-0.8	+0.4	+0.4	-0.1	+0.0	+0.1
Estimated total impact of SMP	-4.2	+2.1	+2.0	-1.2	-0.4	+1.7	-2.3	+0.5	+1.8
Total actual change, 1991-94	-3.7	+1.0	+2.7	-2.3	-0.1	+2.4	-2.8	+0.3	+2.5

Such widespread reductions in price margins provide strong evidence that some of the supply-side effects of the single market appear to be operating. We are not able to detect whether this is through the direct reductions in price-cost margins or whether it is a result of improvements in X-efficiency.

Table 4.6 summarizes our results for the 15 different industries included in this study analysed by country. Analysing our results by country is potentially misleading because of the considerable differences in industrial structure between EU countries. The results for the 15 industries studied, however, show that in all the principal countries price-cost margins have contracted. The main difference in country experience is in the behaviour of market shares. In Germany domestic market shares on average rise, with a corresponding fall taking place in other EU countries' exports to those markets. In contrast, in France, Italy, and the UK domestic market share tends to fall, and both EU and non-EU import shares are stimulated.

To obtain the full effects of the single market policies on trade flows we have considered the overall effects of demand and supply factors combined. The impact of the increased competition in EU domestic markets and reduced price-cost margins has been simulated using our estimated results for both demand and price equations.

Table 4.6.   Estimated impacts of the SMP: results by country for 15 sectors

	Number of observations	Estimated price competition impact on price-cost margins (%)	Estimated direct demand impact (%)		
			Home	EU	RoW
D	15	-1.4	+1.8	-2.9	+1.1
F	15	-9.4	-8.2	+4.3	+3.9
I	15	-4.3	-11.2	+7.7	+3.5
UK	13	-2.9	-4.6	+1.6	+3.0
Average of large countries		-3.9	-5.3	+2.9	+2.4

In general, taking into account the competitiveness effects tends to raise the market share of domestic producers. EU importer shares tend to fall since the major competitiveness effects on prices occur mainly in previously protected net importer markets. Non-EU importer shares are reduced by the competitiveness effects. The results suggest that the overall shifts in trade shares are overestimated by the use of the traditional direct effects analysis. In the 15 most sensitive sectors, taking into account the competition impact tends to lower our estimate of the impact of the SMP on domestic market shares. In the sensitive sectors on average, improved price-cost margins are estimated to have restored domestic market shares by 1.2%, roughly a quarter of our estimate of the reduction caused by direct demand effects. EU and non-EU importers lose market share in roughly equal proportions. The simulation results demonstrate that it is essential to consider the supply-side effects of the SMP on increasing competition to obtain a full evaluation of the programme. The results suggest that the overall shifts in trade shares are overestimated by the use of the traditional direct effects analysis.

Our estimates of the overall impact of the SMP taking into account both demand and competition effects, suggest that the programme has been strongly trade creating. The overall impact on domestic market shares is estimated to have been 4.2% in the 15 sensitive sectors and 2.3% in manufacturing as a whole.

It is also clear that there is little evidence of trade diversion. The overall impact of the SMP is estimated to have increased extra-EU import shares by 2.0% in the 15 sensitive sectors and by 1.8% in overall manufacturing.

The extent of the overall SMP impact on intra-EU trade is affected by the under-recording of trade flows between EU states as a result of the introduction of the INTRASTAT system. Nevertheless, even using the published data, we estimate that the SMP has increased intra-EU imports by 2.1% in the 15 sensitive sectors and by 0.5% in manufacturing as a whole. These effects are almost certainly considerably underestimated.

5. Computable general equilibrium analysis

5.1. Introduction

As described in detail in Chapter 2 and its Technical Appendix, the computable general equilibrium (CGE) model operates at the three-digit level, but with more comprehensive sectoral coverage than the econometric model, and it, too, models producers as imperfectly competitive firms operating in markets with differentiated products. As a fully specified general equilibrium model of trade and production, the CGE model is more elaborate than the econometric model, allowing a richer set of linkages between markets (notably linkages between sectors through the labour markets), but whereas the parameters of the econometric model are estimated on the basis of data series spanning several years, the parameters of the CGE model are imposed, some on the basis of estimates from the literature, and the rest so that the numerical solution of the model reproduces the data of the single base year of 1991.

In this chapter we report on the results of three different exercises. The first exercise undertaken with the CGE model is an ex-ante simulation, where estimates made in 1990 of the likely effects of the SMP on intra-EU trade costs were imposed on the model and the effects on the equilibrium re-computed. This exercise serves to highlight the changes in production that were anticipated in 1990, and these can then be compared to the actual changes.

However, as the main focus of this paper is on highlighting actual effects, we focus our attention on the second exercise. For this exercise we have undertaken ex-post simulations, where the values of the changes in trade costs are chosen so as to reproduce as an equilibrium the changes in market shares observed between 1991 and 1994. Two types of ex-post simulation are undertaken, one in which only intra-EU trade barriers are changed, the other in which extra-EU trade barriers are changed to the same extent as intra-EU barriers.

For the ex-ante exercise we report on the results of a short-run simulation in which markets are segmented (that is to say, firms can set prices independently in each national market of the EU), firm numbers are fixed, but wages are allowed to adjust. For the ex-post exercise, (i) we detail the effects of a short-run simulation as in the ex-ante case; (ii) in order to capture changes in competitive behaviour by firms, we maintain the short-run assumptions and do not allow price-cost margins to change. The comparison, therefore, between (i) and (ii) enables us to assess the extent to which changes in firms' pricing behaviour impacts on market shares; (iii) finally the long-run effects of the SMP are modelled by supposing that firms start to treat the whole EU as a single market, and that entry and exit of producers will take place. Finally, we also report results on the changes in GDP and welfare across countries as well as the changes in factor demands.

5.2. Calibration

The numerical specification of the CGE model is undertaken first by setting some key parameters, notably those describing demand elasticities and returns to scale on the basis of literature estimates, and then calculating the values of remaining parameters and endogenous variables so that the base year observations support an equilibrium.

The price elasticity of demand for the industry aggregates are assumed to be one. The price elasticities of demand for individual varieties depend on the elasticities of substitution in the

CES aggregators. We assume that this elasticity of substitution is the same for all industries, and is equal to 10 for final products and to 5 for intermediate products.

For final products we assume that the base data set represents a long-run equilibrium in which profits are zero. Technology and firm scale imply a relationship between average cost and marginal cost, and, with the assumption of long-run equilibrium, this also gives a relationship between price and marginal cost. This price-cost margin is supported at equilibrium by two considerations: product differentiation and market power stemming from the degree of concentration in the industry and the form of interaction between firms. We assume that the base case is a segmented market Cournot equilibrium. The number of varieties and the output per variety are then chosen so that the degree of product differentiation implied by the assumed elasticity of substitution is compatible with the assumed scale economies. The final stage of calibration involves positioning demand curves so that consumption of products in each country is consistent with the matrix of production and consumption.

5.3. Data

As described previously, the model has 12 countries, three factors of production, a perfectly competitive sector and a number of imperfectly competitive sectors based on the NACE three-digit classification. At the three-digit level there are 118 manufacturing industries. This number is first reduced by resolving some incompatibilities in the NACE classifications between trade and industrial statistics. Further, because of data limitations in certain countries in small industries, it was necessary to introduce some aggregation, and the model works with 64 imperfectly competitive sectors which are listed in Table 5.1.

The trade data were obtained from the COMEXT databank, and the production data primarily from the VISA database. At the three-digit level, the VISA database for any given year is not complete. A variety of procedures have been employed in order to complete the data set. Where data were available for an earlier year, the overall change in manufacturing production between the earlier year and 1991 was used to interpolate a production figure; the INDE database provided some of the missing data; and finally, where no production data were available, the average production/export ratio for those countries for which data were available was taken in order to interpolate a production figure on the basis of the reported trade flows.

Data on concentration, firm numbers and returns to scale are obtained from the study carried out by Davies and Lyons [1996] and from the survey by Pratten [1988]. In a model based on imperfect competition, data on concentration are crucial, and compared with the work done by Gasiorek, Smith and Venables [1992], the availability of concentration data from the recent work of Lyons *et al.* – collected on an EU-wide basis and in a way that is more satisfactory than national census data – should considerably improve the reliability of the model. For each sector, Davies and Lyons report a Herfindahl-equivalent number of firms in a Herfindahl-typical EU country, and it is the market share implied by this statistic which we have entered into our imperfectly competitive pricing equations in describing market concentration in the base equilibrium.

Table 5.1.   Sectoral disaggregation

NACE		NACE	
22	Metals	361:363,365	Ships, rail stock, cycles
23	Mineral extraction	364	Aerospace
241:244	Clay, cement, asbestos	37	Instruments
245:248	Stone, glass, ceramics	411,420:423	Grains, pasta, bread
251	Basic chemicals	412	Other foods
255	Paint and ink	413	Meat products
256	Industrial & agricultural chemicals	414	Dairy products
257	Pharmaceuticals	415	Fruit and vegetable products
258	Soap and detergents	416:419	Fish products
259	Domestic chemicals	424:428	Drinks
260	Man-made fibres	429	Tobacco
311:313	Metal manufacture	43A	Wool, cotton, silk, flax
314:315	Metal structures, boilers	436	Knitting
316	Tools and cans	438	Carpets
321	Tractors & agricultural machinery	439	Miscellaneous textiles
322	Machine tools	441	Leather tanning
323	Textile machinery	442	Leather products
324	Food and chemical machinery	451	Footwear
325	Mining and construction machinery	453	Clothing
326	Transmission equipment	455:456	Household textiles, fur
327	Paper and wood machinery	461:462	Wood boards
328	Other machinery	463:465	Other wood
330	Computers and office machinery	466	Cork and brushes
341	Insulated wires and cables	467	Wooden furniture
342	Electrical machinery	471	Paper and pulp
343	Electrical equipment	472	Processed paper
344	Telecoms and measuring equipment	473	Print and publishing
345	Radio and TV	481:482	Rubber
346	Domestic electrical appliances	483	Plastics
347	Electric lighting	491	Jewellery
351	Motor vehicles	492:493	Musical instruments, photos
352:353	Motor vehicle parts	494	Toys and sports

Davies and Lyons also used Pratten's estimates of scale economies in their econometric work, although there are some minor differences for some sectors between the numbers we have derived from Pratten for the cost disadvantage of sub-optimal scales of production and those used by Davies and Lyons.

Other required industry-specific data include the share of value added in production; the share of each factor in value added; the elasticity of substitution between different factors of production; and the share of final demand in the output of each industry. The principal source for most of these data is the VISA database, with other data derived from supplementary sources such as INDE and published Eurostat data.

A listing of the sectoral names is given in Table 5.1, and Table 5.2 then gives relevant sectoral data. Column 1 of the table lists the average degree of concentration in that industry in Europe as reported by Davies and Lyons. The figure reported here is a Herfindahl index (HNAT in their terminology), the reciprocal of which gives the number of equivalent-sized firms. The most concentrated industries are 347 (electrical lamps and other electrical lighting equipment), 260 (man-made fibres), 259 (household and office chemicals), 429 (tobacco products), 351 (motor vehicles), 364 (aerospace), 373 (optical instruments) and 330 (office machinery). The least concentrated industries are 433 (silk), 464 (wooden containers), 313 (metal treatment), 453 (ready-made clothing), 467 (wooden furniture), and 465 (other wood).

The second column of Table 5.2 gives the share of value added in each industry with the highest share of value added reported in 22 (production and preliminary processing of metal), the lowest in 321 (agricultural machinery and tractors), and where the average share across all industries is 0.36. The third, fourth and fifth columns give the share of capital, non-manual labour and manual labour respectively in each industry. The most capital intensive sectors are 429 (tobacco products), 424:428 (drinks), 23 (mineral extraction), 416:419 (grain, pasta, starch, bread), 256 (other industrial chemical products), and 257 (pharmaceutical products). The non-manual labour intensive industries are 364 (aerospace), 321 (agricultural machinery), 323 (textile machinery), 330 (office machinery), 344 (telecoms equipment). Finally the most manual labour intensive industries are 451 (footwear), 455:456 (household textiles, furs), 463:465 (various wood products), 466 (cork and articles of straw) and 467 (wooden furniture).

The next column of Table 5.2 lists the degree of economies of scale in each industry. In the majority of cases the percentage figure refers to the increase in costs as a result of a 50% reduction in output from the minimum efficient scale of output. For those industries with an asterisk the figure relates to the increase in costs arising from a 33% reduction in output from the minimum efficient scale; and for those with a double asterisk a 67% reduction. These estimates are engineering estimates for which the primary data source was Pratten [1988]. Because of the differences in the measurement methods, it is not straightforward to rank industries by their degree of scale economies, but among those where economies of scale are highest are 241:244 (clay products, cement lime and plaster, asbestos), 251, 256, 257, 259 (chemicals industries), 341, 342 (electrical cables and machinery), 351, 352, 353 (motor vehicles and accessories), 364 (aerospace), and 37 (instrument engineering).

In the next two sections we report the results of the two exercises. In all simulations we allow for the flexibility of factor prices, but we make different assumptions about the free entry and exit of firms, the size of the change associated with the single market programme and the nature of firms' responses.

Table 5.2. Industry characteristics

Industry	Conc.	V.A. share	Share in value added			Returns to scale	NTB	Vuln	BIL 20	MA 20
			Capital	Non-manual labour	Manual labour					
22	0.17	0.28	0.25	0.48	0.27	1.11*	1.00	0.00		
23	0.10	0.50	0.45	0.33	0.22	1.11*	1.00	0.00		
241:244	0.04	0.44	0.37	0.45	0.17	1.25*	2.00	0.00		
245:248	0.06	0.44	0.27	0.46	0.27	1.11*	1.75	0.50	✓	
251	0.07	0.31	0.38	0.53	0.10	1.15	1.00	1.00	✓	✓
255	0.21	0.35	0.36	0.54	0.10	1.04*	1.00	0.00		
256	0.11	0.39	0.40	0.50	0.09	1.15	2.00	1.00	✓	✓
257	0.07	0.41	0.40	0.50	0.09	1.15	3.00	3.00	✓	✓
258	0.06	0.30	0.39	0.52	0.10	1.02	2.00	0.00		✓
259	0.40	0.37	0.34	0.55	0.10	1.15	2.00	0.00		✓
260	0.47	0.32	0.25	0.51	0.24	1.10	1.00	0.00		
311:313	0.02	0.43	0.26	0.43	0.32	1.07	1.00	0.00		
314:315	0.01	0.42	0.21	0.55	0.24	1.07	2.50	1.50	✓	
316	0.01	0.40	0.30	0.47	0.23	1.07	1.00	0.00		
321	0.05	0.35	0.15	0.64	0.22	1.07	2.00	1.00		
322	0.02	0.47	0.19	0.61	0.21	1.07	2.00	1.00	✓	
323	0.04	0.41	0.16	0.63	0.21	1.07	2.00	1.00		
324	0.03	0.43	0.27	0.55	0.19	1.07	2.00	1.00	✓	
325	0.03	0.36	0.23	0.58	0.20	1.07	2.00	1.00	✓	
326	0.05	0.47	0.20	0.60	0.20	1.09*	2.00	1.00		
327	0.03	0.41	0.25	0.56	0.19	1.07	2.00	1.00		
328	0.05	0.39	0.24	0.57	0.19	1.10	2.00	0.00		
330	0.27	0.44	0.34	0.61	0.05	1.07*	3.00	4.00	✓	✓
341	0.03	0.31	0.30	0.56	0.14	1.15	3.00	2.00	✓	✓
342	0.02	0.41	0.25	0.60	0.15	1.15	3.00	2.00	✓	✓
343	0.10	0.39	0.25	0.60	0.15	1.05*	1.00	0.00		✓
344	0.05	0.45	0.24	0.61	0.15	1.1*	3.00	4.00	✓	
345	0.06	0.34	0.27	0.59	0.14	1.1*	2.00	1.00	✓	✓
346	0.18	0.35	0.27	0.59	0.14	1.07*	2.00	1.00		
347	0.47	0.40	0.30	0.56	0.14	1.10	2.00	1.00		
351	0.33	0.25	0.20	0.49	0.31	1.15*	2.00	1.00	✓	
352:353	0.08	0.36	0.22	0.47	0.30	1.15*	2.00	0.00		
361:363, 365	0.15	0.36	0.17	0.50	0.33	1.08	2.33	1.67		✓
364	0.29	0.40	0.19	0.69	0.13	1.15*	2.00	1.00	✓	✓
37	0.09	0.48	0.27	0.57	0.16	1.15	1.50	1.00		✓
411, 420:423	0.07	0.26	0.29	0.50	0.21	1.06**	1.40	0.40		
412	0.01	0.17	0.30	0.49	0.21	1.05**	1.00	0.00		
413	0.03	0.17	0.39	0.43	0.18	1.02**	1.00	0.00		
414	0.02	0.25	0.40	0.42	0.18	1.08**	1.00	0.00		
415	0.08	0.23	0.31	0.49	0.21	1.05**	1.00	0.00		
416:419	0.05	0.27	0.44	0.39	0.17	1.08**	1.50	0.50		✓
424:428	0.08	0.40	0.48	0.39	0.13	1.07*	2.50	2.25	✓	✓
429	0.35	0.16	0.59	0.27	0.14	1.02*	1.00	0.00		
43A,B	0.02	0.42	0.24	0.46	0.30	1.03	1.50	0.50	✓	
436	0.01	0.37	0.28	0.41	0.32	1.03	2.00	0.00		
438	0.05	0.33	0.34	0.40	0.26	1.10	2.00	1.00		
439	0.05	0.41	0.34	0.40	0.26	1.03	2.00	0.00		
441	0.01	0.26	0.32	0.38	0.30	1.03	1.00	0.00		✓
442	0.01	0.41	0.25	0.42	0.33	1.03	1.00	0.00		✓

Table 5.2.   Industry characteristics (continued)

Industry	Conc.	V.A. share	Share in value added			Returns to scale	NTB	Vuln	BIL 20	MA 20
			Capital	Non-manual labour	Manual labour					
451	0.01	0.38	0.25	0.36	0.39	1.01*	2.00	1.00		
453	0.00	0.34	0.25	0.43	0.32	1.03	2.00	1.00	✓	
455:456	0.01	0.35	0.19	0.46	0.35	1.03	1.50	0.50		✓
461:462	0.02	0.35	0.30	0.39	0.32	1.05	1.50	0.00		
463:465	0.01	0.40	0.23	0.43	0.35	1.05	1.33	0.00		
466	0.03	0.41	0.25	0.41	0.34	1.05	1.00	0.00		
467	0.00	0.37	0.25	0.41	0.34	1.05	1.00	0.00		
471	0.03	0.33	0.40	0.37	0.23	1.10	1.00	0.00		
472	0.02	0.33	0.31	0.46	0.23	1.10	1.00	0.00		
473	0.02	0.45	0.26	0.57	0.18	1.13	1.00	0.00		
481:482	0.16	0.45	0.31	0.45	0.24	1.05	2.00	1.00	✓	✓
483	0.01	0.37	0.34	0.46	0.21	1.05	2.00	0.00		
491	0.01	0.39	0.24	0.50	0.26	1.05	2.00	1.00		
492:493	0.03	0.46	0.20	0.53	0.27	1.05	1.50	0.50		
494	0.06	0.37	0.35	0.43	0.22	1.05	2.00	0.00		✓

*   Figure relates to the increase in costs arising from a 33% reduction in output from the minimum efficient scale.

**   Figure relates to the increase in costs arising from a 67% reduction in output from the minimum efficient scale.

5.4.   The ex-ante simulation

In the first simulation we assume that the SMP reduces the costs of intra-European trade but that firms still act as if the markets in Europe were segmented. This means that firms set marginal revenue equal to marginal cost separately in each market (country) in which they operate. The size of the experiment is based on the Buigues, Ilzkovitz and Lebrun [1990] (referred to below as BIL [1990]) estimates of the sectoral impact of the SMP, and uses the same numbers (aggregation aside) as Davies and Lyons. Columns 7 and 8 of Table 5.2 show respectively the extent to which the sector was affected by non-tariff barriers to intra-EU trade (NTB), and the vulnerability of the sector to other SMP measures, particularly with respect to public procurement (Vuln). The former variable ranges between 1 and 3, the latter between 0 and 4. We have assumed an effect of the SMP equivalent to a reduction in an *ad valorem* tariff on intra-EU trade of 1% multiplied by the sum of these two variables, so the tariff equivalent is a 1% reduction in sectors such as 412-415 (which are food products sectors) and ranges up to a 7% reduction in 330 (office machinery) and 344 (telecommunications equipment).

The results for manufacturing in aggregate are reported in Table 5.3, and the detailed results by country and by sector are reported in Table A5.1 in the unpublished Appendix to this chapter. Following on the discussion in Chapter 2, the results we report for each industry are:

(a)   Columns 1 to 3 report on the base consumption shares. These are the share of domestic production in domestic consumption (Home), the share of EU imports in domestic consumption (EU), and the share of non-EU imports in domestic consumption (RoW). This information is included here in order to give a sense of the scale of the changes reported in the first three columns.

(b)   Columns 4 to 6 give the change in consumption shares for each country. The changes are reported in percentages. Hence if a domestic market share (Home) fell from 40% to 36%, the number reported in the first column of the table would be -4%.

(c)   The final column gives the percentage change in the share of EU imports in domestic consumption.

Table 5.3.   Change in trade patterns, all manufacturing – ex-ante simulation

	Base shares			Change in shares (%)			% change in EU share
	Home	EU	RoW	Home	EU	RoW	
F	76.75	16.05	7.19	-2.55	2.99	-0.44	1.19
D	75.6	13.58	10.82	-2.28	2.83	-0.55	1.21
I	79.53	13.41	7.07	-2.15	2.5	-0.35	1.19
UK	74.19	14.48	11.32	-2.25	2.88	-0.63	1.2
NL	62.63	25.7	11.67	-2.32	3.42	-1.1	1.13
B-L	58.34	31.21	10.45	-2.47	3.59	-1.11	1.11
DK	63.75	21.69	14.55	-1.85	3.05	-1.21	1.14
IRL	71.53	20.34	8.13	-2.04	2.72	-0.68	1.13
GR	73.29	18.47	8.24	-1.4	2.13	-0.73	1.12
E	77.55	16.45	6	-2.35	2.78	-0.43	1.17
P	72.54	21.74	5.71	-1.6	2.29	-0.69	1.11

Rather than providing a detailed description of the changes by industry and country, we first focus on the broad pattern of results and then move on to highlight certain key changes in particular sectors.

The results are shown for individual countries, and differences between countries will primarily reflect differences in the production structures between countries. However, it is not these differences on which one should focus in interpreting the table, but rather the common pattern of the results. In almost each case the Home share declines by just over 2%, the EU share increases by around 3% and the RoW share declines by less than 1%. In terms of the standard terminology, of the increase in intra-EU trade, two thirds is trade creation and one third trade diversion. The fall in the RoW share indicates that the increased intra-EU market access generated by the SMP is partially at the expense of the shares of producers from the rest of the world.

This pattern of change is in general reflected in the individual industry results which are reported in detail in Table A5.1 (unpublished). The Home share goes down for every industry and every country, as does the RoW share, while the EU share goes up in every case. There is, however, unsurprisingly, a fairly wide variation in the extent of these changes. For example, the largest changes are experienced in 342 (electrical machinery), 414 (fruit and vegetable products), 438 (carpets), as well as generally in the machinery industry (322-328), whereas the smallest changes are to be found, for example, in 260 (artificial and synthetic fibres) or 429 (tobacco).

There are a number of explanations for the differences in results across industries. Clearly, the difference in the size of simulated experiment is very important. However, the results are not proportional to the size of the sectoral simulation, but are clearly also influenced by the base pattern of trade. Where a very high proportion of the market is supplied by domestic producers both trade creation and trade diversion tend to be low. Conversely, the lower the share of the market supplied by domestic producers, the higher will be trade creation and trade diversions. Equally, the division between trade creation and trade diversion can, to some extent, be understood by looking at the base shares. Where the share of imports from the EU is higher, the more likely it is that there will be trade creation; the higher the share from the rest of the world relative to the EU share, the more likely it is that the ratio of trade diversion to trade creation will be higher.

These results seem to be driven by simple economic arithmetic: if foreign and partner producers have a small market share, intra-EU trade cost reductions have their direct impact on a small base number, so home market shares are only a little reduced, and there is little third-country trade to squeeze; while if much trade is already taking place, the improved access for EU partner producers may affect third-country producers as much as home producers.

The detailed sectoral tables illustrate these results. As reported above, the largest changes in trade costs are in industries 330 (office machinery) and 344 (telecommunications equipment). However, these industries do not experience the largest changes. Indeed, industry 344 experiences comparatively small changes. This can be understood by looking at the base shares. For many of the countries, industry 344 has a high domestic share in consumption (e.g. up to 89% for Germany). Industry 414, which has the largest changes, also has low shares in domestic consumption. Those industries with the smallest changes (such as industries 260, 429, 416, 463, and 473) all have high shares in domestic consumption.

One might also expect that the larger the economies of scale in an industry, the more likely it is that firms can take advantage of those economies of scale as market access barriers are lowered. However, it is hard to discern such a pattern, given the strong effect already identified of base market shares.

5.5. The ex-post simulation with no direct effects on external trade

In this section, we continue to assume that the SMP reduces the costs of intra-European trade. However, we now select the trade cost reductions in an entirely different way. We continue to suppose that the SMP reduces only intra-EU trade costs, and that the level of that reduction differs between sectors but is the same for all EU countries. We find which are the trade cost reductions that would bring about the actual increase in the intra-EU trade share (averaged across EU countries) which occurred between 1991 and 1994, when the model is run without entry or exit of producers.

On the basis of this we then report the results of three simulations. First, the change in trade costs described above can then be used to run a base simulation which replicates the actual change in shares that occurred between 1991 to 1994, and details the concomitant changes in patterns of trade. Second, in order to capture the effect of possible changes in competitive behaviour by firms, we run the same simulation but now hold price-cost margins fixed. The difference between the two simulations then gives an estimate of the extent to which changes in firms' behaviour may have impacted upon market shares and hence upon trade patterns. Finally, the full effects of the SMP are simulated by running the model with these trade cost reductions, but allowing labour market adjustment and entry and exit of firms and assuming EU markets are integrated, so firms cannot price discriminate between national markets.

The basis for this group of simulations (the actual change in shares between 1991 and 1994) effectively makes the assumption that all of the trade change over this period is to be explained by the response of (a fixed number of existing) firms to the SMP, and this clearly is a rather extreme assumption, which will give a maximalist estimate of the long-run effects of the SMP. However, in some sectors the intra-EU trade share actually falls in the period 1991-94, and rather than assume that the SMP has had the perverse effect of raising intra-EU trade barriers in these sectors, we have set the change in trade barriers to zero in these cases.

Detailed below in Table 5.4 are the changes in shares for each of the countries, and for three different aggregations of our 64 manufacturing sectors. The first part of the table details the changes for the sum of all of the sectors ('All manufacturing'). Following on from the selection of industries in Chapter 4, the second part of the table aggregates the results for the 20 most sensitive sectors as identified by BIL [1990] with the highest shares of value added. These sectors are identified in the last but one column of Table 5.2, labelled BIL-20. Finally, the last section of the table aggregates the results for the 20 industries which, over the period 1991-94, have experienced the largest change in the share of imports from the EU. These sectors are identified in the last column of Table 5.2, labelled MA-20.

The columns of the table are as in Table 5.3. There are now, however, four additional columns which give the results of the second simulation which we call the competition effect. Columns 1 to 3 list the base shares in domestic consumption; columns 4 to 6 the change in shares arising from the base simulation, and column 7 the percentage change in the EU share in domestic consumption. It is worth noting that the average of this share across the EU countries represents the actual average percentage change in shares which occurred between 1991 and 1994.

Columns 8 to 10 detail how the base change in shares would have been affected if firms were unable to adjust their behaviour and change price-cost mark-ups. For example, for all manufacturing in the base simulation, France experienced a change in the share of trade coming from the EU of 1.93%. If firms had been unable to adjust their competitive behaviour, the change in the EU share of trade would have been 1.96%. The competition effect has therefore decreased the share of trade by -0.03%, which is the figure reported in column 9. Finally, column 11 reports the percentage change in the EU share in domestic consumption for this second simulation.

Looking first at the change for manufacturing as a whole it can be seen that there is a very consistent pattern of changes across countries. The domestic share declines by approximately 1.5%, the EU share rises on average by 2%, and the share of imports from the rest of the world falls by roughly 0.5%. As in the ex-ante simulation, the size of the impact appears to be closely related to the base share characteristics. The competition effect has in most cases had a small impact on these shares for the major EU economies. In contrast, allowing firms in Greece to adjust their competitive behaviour has reduced the decrease in domestic share by 0.32% (from -1.12 to -0.8)

Turning to the other two sectoral aggregations, the changes are greater for the BIL [1990] sensitive sectors (hereafter referred to as the BIL sectors). The change in the EU share has increased by approximately 1%, with the home share experiencing roughly an addition 0.66% reduction, and the RoW share an additional 0.33% reduction. Finally, by definition the largest changes are experienced in the most affected sectors. The most affected sectors experience changes in shares which are roughly twice the magnitude of manufacturing as a whole.

Table 5.4.   Aggregate changes in trade patterns – ex-post 1

	Base shares			Change in shares: all effects			% Δ in EU share	Change in shares: competition effect			% Δ in EU share
	Home	EU	RoW	Home	EU	RoW		Home	EU	RoW	
All manufacturing											
F	76.75	16.05	7.19	-1.65	1.93	-0.28	1.12	0.04	-0.03	-0.01	1.12
D	75.60	13.58	10.82	-1.36	1.74	-0.38	1.13	0.02	-0.01	0	1.13
I	79.53	13.41	7.07	-1.42	1.68	-0.25	1.13	0.06	-0.05	-0.01	1.13
UK	74.19	14.48	11.32	-1.40	1.87	-0.47	1.13	0.05	-0.04	-0.01	1.13
NL	62.63	25.7	11.67	-1.45	2.18	-0.73	1.08	0.11	-0.10	-0.01	1.09
B-L	58.34	31.21	10.45	-1.55	2.29	-0.74	1.07	0.13	-0.11	-0.02	1.08
DK	63.75	21.69	14.55	-1.06	1.85	-0.78	1.09	0.27	-0.20	-0.06	1.09
IRL	71.53	20.34	8.13	-1.45	1.98	-0.53	1.10	0.26	-0.22	-0.04	1.11
GR	73.29	18.47	8.24	-0.80	1.31	-0.51	1.07	0.32	-0.26	-0.06	1.09
E	77.55	16.45	6.00	-1.43	1.77	-0.34	1.11	0.14	-0.13	-0.01	1.12
P	72.54	21.74	5.71	-0.68	1.19	-0.51	1.05	0.16	-0.15	-0.02	1.06
BIL [1990] sensitive sectors											
F	75.48	16.74	7.78	-2.32	2.66	-0.34	1.16	0.06	-0.05	-0.01	1.16
D	71.39	15.94	12.67	-1.85	2.48	-0.63	1.16	0.03	-0.03	0	1.16
I	74.91	17.62	7.47	-2.14	2.54	-0.40	1.14	0.11	-0.09	-0.02	1.15
UK	66.72	18.95	14.33	-1.94	2.83	-0.89	1.15	0.08	-0.07	0	1.15
NL	64.12	22.57	13.3	-1.81	2.84	-1.03	1.13	0.14	-0.12	-0.02	1.13
B-L	54.22	32.62	13.16	-1.87	3.03	-1.16	1.09	0.15	-0.13	-0.02	1.10
DK	59.73	24.38	15.89	-1.36	2.56	-1.20	1.10	0.40	-0.29	-0.11	1.12
IRL	61.48	23.93	14.58	-2.11	3.22	-1.10	1.13	0.41	-0.32	-0.08	1.15
GR	57.02	30.32	12.66	-1.01	2.17	-1.16	1.07	0.72	-0.56	-0.15	1.09
E	68.57	22.59	8.84	-1.91	2.61	-0.7	1.12	0.15	-0.12	-0.02	1.12
P	60.71	32.63	6.66	-0.97	1.80	-0.83	1.06	0.29	-0.26	-0.03	1.06
Most affected sectors											
F	77.41	13.98	8.61	-2.73	3.23	-0.51	1.23	0.07	-0.06	-0.01	1.24
D	69.65	15.90	14.46	-2.67	3.69	-1.02	1.23	0.06	-0.05	0	1.24
I	74.59	15.70	9.71	-2.99	3.66	-0.67	1.23	0.13	-0.10	-0.02	1.24
UK	67.90	17.07	15.03	-2.84	4.03	-1.20	1.24	0.10	-0.10	-0.01	1.24
NL	69.72	17.90	12.38	-2.64	3.82	-1.18	1.21	0.18	-0.15	-0.02	1.22
B-L	52.54	33.51	13.95	-2.91	4.60	-1.70	1.14	0.30	-0.27	-0.04	1.15
DK	58.54	25.14	16.31	-2.42	4.16	-1.74	1.17	0.68	-0.52	-0.16	1.19
IRL	65.06	20.99	13.95	-2.77	3.99	-1.23	1.19	0.51	-0.42	-0.10	1.21
GR	56.87	24.86	18.27	-1.92	3.66	-1.74	1.15	1.02	-0.82	-0.21	1.18
E	72.36	17.41	10.23	-2.50	3.48	-0.98	1.2	0.19	-0.16	-0.03	1.21
P	65.01	27.21	7.78	-1.84	3.08	-1.24	1.11	0.59	-0.52	-0.07	1.13

Table A5.2 in the unpublished Appendix lists the results for each of the 64 industries. The pattern of effects across sectors is different from the ex-ante simulation, because the trade cost reduction in this case follows a quite different inter-sectoral pattern from the BIL [1990] numbers which were used previously. For a given size of the simulation the results can be understood in the same way as with the ex-ante simulation: larger domestic shares tend to produce smaller changes in shares.

In general the competition effect is small for most industries and countries. However, the following patterns can be discerned. First, the competition effect is usually more important for the smaller countries in the EU. Second, the competition effect becomes more important either when the industry is more concentrated and/or where the returns to scale are higher.

The other interesting point of comparison is with the ex-ante BIL [1990] estimates. Here there are two observations. First, the aggregate results we report in the ex-post simulation are smaller for each country than the results for the ex-ante simulation. This suggests that either we have chosen too large a factor to scale the change in trade costs to the BIL [1990] estimates or that the effects are still to be translated into actual changes in trade flows. Second, while the BIL sectors have experienced a larger change in patterns of trade than manufacturing in aggregate, they have not experienced the largest changes.

Another angle on this comparison is provided by the trade cost changes which are calculated in the first stage of each simulation. The trade cost changes for the ex-ante simulation, and the trade cost changes for the first ex-post simulation are plotted in Figure 5.1. The former is based on the BIL [1990] numbers, the latter on the observed changes in traded shares.

Figure 5.1.   Correlation of changes in trade costs: BIL-1990 and ex-post 1

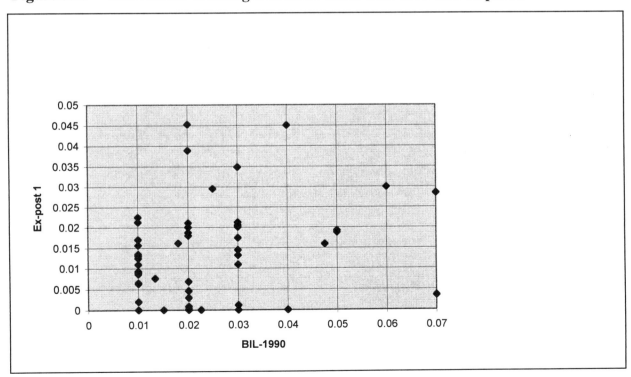

Table 5.5.   Aggregate changes in trade patterns – ex-post 2

	Base shares			Change in shares: base			% Δ in EU share	Change in shares: competition effect			% Δ in EU share
	Home	EU	RoW	Home	EU	RoW		Home	EU	RoW	
All manufacturing											
F	76.75	16.05	7.19	-3.22	2.12	1.11	1.13	0.08	-0.04	-0.02	1.13
D	75.6	13.58	10.82	-2.78	1.63	1.14	1.12	0.04	-0.02	-0.03	1.12
I	79.53	13.41	7.07	-2.7	1.82	0.88	1.14	0.1	-0.07	-0.03	1.14
UK	74.19	14.48	11.32	-2.79	1.7	1.08	1.12	0.08	-0.05	-0.04	1.12
NL	62.63	25.7	11.67	-2.8	1.78	1.02	1.07	0.19	-0.12	-0.06	1.07
B-L	58.34	31.21	10.45	-2.76	1.98	0.77	1.06	0.22	-0.16	-0.07	1.07
DK	63.75	21.69	14.55	-2.36	1.4	0.96	1.06	0.55	-0.34	-0.21	1.08
IRL	71.53	20.34	8.13	-2.58	1.74	0.84	1.09	0.48	-0.34	-0.15	1.1
GR	73.29	18.47	8.24	-1.46	0.92	0.54	1.05	0.61	-0.4	-0.21	1.07
E	77.55	16.45	6	-2.41	1.74	0.67	1.11	0.21	-0.16	-0.05	1.12
P	72.54	21.74	5.71	-1.31	1.03	0.28	1.05	0.3	-0.24	-0.06	1.06
BIL [1990] sensitive sectors											
F	75.48	16.74	7.78	-0.26	0.52	-0.26	0.98	4.84	-3.1	-1.74	1.19
D	71.39	15.94	12.67	-4.73	3.03	1.7	1.18	-0.99	0.8	0.2	1.14
I	74.91	17.62	7.47	-3.67	2.21	1.46	1.14	0.6	-0.74	0.14	1.17
UK	66.72	18.95	14.33	-4.07	2.81	1.26	1.16	0.05	0.39	-0.44	1.13
NL	64.12	22.57	13.3	-3.98	2.34	1.64	1.12	0.37	-0.14	-0.23	1.11
B-L	54.22	32.62	13.16	-4.07	2.32	1.75	1.1	-0.05	-0.35	0.4	1.08
DK	59.73	24.38	15.89	-3.72	2.47	1.25	1.08	0.07	0.08	-0.16	1.1
IRL	61.48	23.93	14.58	-2.92	1.84	1.08	1.08	2.28	-1.35	-0.92	1.13
GR	57.02	30.32	12.66	-4.35	2.65	1.69	1.11	-1.22	0.51	0.7	1.07
E	68.57	22.59	8.84	-1.78	1.23	0.55	1.04	1.88	-1.35	-0.53	1.11
P	60.71	32.63	6.66	-3.39	2.4	1	1.11	-1.18	0.62	0.57	1.05
Most affected sectors											
F	77.41	13.98	8.61	-1.72	1.39	0.33	1.04	6.28	-3.71	-2.57	1.27
D	69.65	15.9	14.46	-6.13	3.62	2.52	1.26	0.35	0.36	-0.7	1.2
I	74.59	15.7	9.71	-6.35	3.2	3.15	1.2	0.58	-0.95	0.38	1.26
UK	67.9	17.07	15.03	-6.65	3.98	2.67	1.25	-0.31	0.49	-0.17	1.2
NL	69.72	17.9	12.38	-6.14	3.39	2.75	1.2	-0.04	-0.13	0.16	1.2
B-L	52.54	33.51	13.95	-5.76	3.31	2.44	1.19	0.51	-0.76	0.24	1.12
DK	58.54	25.14	16.31	-5.68	3.67	2.01	1.11	1.74	-0.33	-1.41	1.16
IRL	65.06	20.99	13.95	-5.96	3.11	2.85	1.12	0.76	-1.08	0.32	1.2
GR	56.87	24.86	18.27	-5.68	3.52	2.16	1.17	0.8	0.08	-0.88	1.14
E	72.36	17.41	10.23	-4.36	2.17	2.19	1.09	1.18	-1.26	0.08	1.2
P	65.01	27.21	7.78	-5.16	3.19	1.97	1.18	-0.84	-0.09	0.92	1.12

Overall, the BIL-derived numbers represent a larger simulation than the ex-post simulation – more of the numbers would lie below than above a 45° line in Figure 5.1: 48 out of the 64, in fact. The largest individual simulations are those based on the BIL numbers: the largest BIL-based reduction in trade costs is 0.07, while for the ex-post simulation the largest reduction is 0.045. This indicates that we have simply chosen too large a scaling factor in the ex-ante simulation. However, it is not the case that the BIL-derived numbers are uniformly larger than the ex-post changes. On the contrary, the scattering of points in the figure has the important implication that the sectoral distribution of the effects of the SMP appears to have been significantly different from that predicted in 1990.

5.6. The ex-post simulation with direct external effects

Both of the previous simulations reduced only intra-EU trade costs and inevitably had the consequence of implying a reduction in the share of extra-EU imports. However, as we saw in Chapters 3 and 4, in reality there have been general increases in the extra-EU import share. In an attempt to capture this effect, we have modelled a second ex-post simulation, in which there is a reduction in extra-EU trade costs as well as in intra-EU trade costs, where the reduction in trade costs is exactly the same for both intra and extra EU trade. The size of the changes in trade costs in each sector are chosen to reproduce as a short-run equilibrium the actual change in the average intra-EU trade share. Again in this case, we set the trade cost change to zero in those cases where the actual changes in market shares would have implied an increase in trade barriers.

The results of the simulations based on these trade cost reductions are set out in Table 5.5 and differ from the previous simulation in the predictable way of encouraging the growth of extra-EU imports, so the extra-EU import share rises in many sectors in many countries, and the domestic share declines to a much greater extent. The greater decline in the domestic share affects the market power of firms in their home markets and so gives larger competition effects, as shown both in the aggregate tables above, and in the detailed tables in Table A5.3 (unpublished). The second ex-post simulation does better than the first in reproducing the changing pattern of EU trade, which points to another important lesson of this exercise: there have been more influences on the trade pattern than a simple reduction in intra-EU barriers. Specifically, it seems that there have been liberalizing forces on external trade that are at least as strong as the intra-EU effects of the SMP.

5.7. Integrated markets

Smith and Venables [1988] identified a key issue in the economics of the SMP as being whether it would induce a change in market conduct, and Table A5.4 in the unpublished Appendix reports the result of the same change in trade costs as in Tables A5.2 and A5.3 (unpublished), but now with firms also switching to an integrated market pricing rule, where it is their market share across the whole EU that determines their price-cost mark-ups in each market. This is a strongly pro-competitive assumption. The assumption that markets remain completely segmented is perhaps too cautious (Sleuwagen and Yamawaki [1988]); but the assumption that the SMP goes all the way to a truly single market may be too bold; so the segmented markets and integrated markets simulations could be regarded as providing bounds somewhere within which it might be reasonable to suppose the truth to lie.

It turns out that in many sectors, the results of imposing the integrated markets assumption produce very large changes in the smaller EU markets – the upper bound of plausibility is too high to be useful, because the effect of a switch from segmented to integrated markets implies in a small EU country an implausibly dramatic change in firms' conduct. We therefore report integrated markets results only for the four largest EU countries.

There are now some significant changes in behaviour compared with the earlier simulation. First, the effects on third-country shares are bigger. We also see cases (sectors 255, 259, 341, for example) where some EU producers' shares fall and some home producers' shares rise. This reflects the fact that a shift to integrated market tends to reduce intra-EU trade. With segmented markets, the large market shares of home firms allow them to set high price-cost margins, which encourages intra-EU imports (as in the 'reciprocal dumping' model of trade). Market integration removes the effect of home market bias on firms' behaviour, and firms cut price-cost mark-ups particularly in their home markets, thus increasing their market shares and driving down imports. We would expect this effect to be stronger in the sectors with higher concentration, and indeed we observe a close link between sectors in which EU partner firms' shares fall and the degree of concentration – 347, 260, 259, 429, 364 are all sectors with high concentration in which home market shares rise sufficiently to drive down EU partner shares in some countries. There are some high concentration sectors in which partner shares do not fall, and some sectors in which partner shares do fall even though concentration is not particularly high, but nevertheless the association is strong.

What these results suggest therefore, is that the pattern of trade creation/diversion and the effects of integration on competitiveness may depend on what the effects of the SMP are on market conduct.

5.8. Economy-wide effects

In this section we move away from the sectoral discussion and report on the results of our simulations at the aggregate level for each country. We focus on identifying the changes that might have taken place in the period 1991-94 and so report on the results of our segmented markets simulations. We present results for welfare and GDP in Table 5.6 and results on employment in Table 5.7.

Table 5.6.   Changes in GDP and welfare – ex-post 1 and ex-post 2

	F	D	I	UK	NL	B-L	DK	IRL	GR	E	P
Ex-post 1	Segmented markets										
% change in GDP	2	2	2	3	3	4	2	4	5	3	9
Change in welfare:											
as % of GDP	2.25	2.42	2.2	2.75	3.71	4.53	2.34	4.03	5.03	3.34	10.07
as % of manuf. VA	8.65	7.58	7.29	9.73	14.2	16.52	11.59	12.24	19.53	10.99	27.62
Ex-post 2	Segmented markets										
% change in GDP	2	2.2	1.9	2.4	3.2	4	2	3.3	4.2	2.8	8.6
Change in welfare:											
as % of GDP	2.27	2.47	2.22	2.8	3.74	4.55	2.36	3.96	5.04	3.35	10.02
as % of manuf. VA	8.72	7.74	7.33	9.9	14.34	16.59	11.68	12.03	19.59	11.05	27.49

Table 5.6 shows the SMP increasing GDP by approximately 2% for each of the four large EU economies, and by more than that for the remaining economies. The largest GDP changes are experienced by Greece and Portugal, and are implausibly large. The scale of these changes is of course reflected in the change in welfare numbers. There is little difference in these effects across the two types of simulations.

For employment, we report the simulated impact on factor demands, both in the base simulation, and in an additional simulation designed to give a quantitative measure of the possible impact on labour markets, by holding factor prices fixed.

Table 5.7 shows that there are differences in the two ex-post simulations. In ex-post 1 all factors in manufacturing experience an increase in demand (capital is assumed to be available on the world market at a constant price, and the changes in labour demand are arrived at through concomitant adjustment in the perfectly competitive sector), with the greatest increase in demand being for manual labour. In contrast, in the second ex-post simulation there is generally a smaller increase in factor demands, particularly for both types of labour. If we take the fixed wages cases as simulating the impact effect of the SMP on employment, then the model indicates that the effects are almost all between 1% and 3% of employment in manufacturing.

Table 5.7.   Change in factor demands (%) – segmented markets

	F	D	I	UK	NL	B-L	DK	IRE	GR	E	P
Ex-post 1 – base											
Capital	1.7	1.87	1.35	2	4.09	5.24	3.22	5.26	2.97	1.73	7.85
Non-manual labour	1.39	1.62	1.1	1.54	3.12	4.12	2.71	4.03	2.26	1.46	6.12
Manual labour	1.83	2.01	1.54	1.73	3.94	5.24	3.27	5.1	2.65	2.01	8.19
Wages fixed											
Capital	1.48	1.63	1.25	1.71	2.63	3.01	2.14	3.6	2.1	1.56	4.87
Non-manual labour	1.56	1.77	1.31	1.72	2.64	3.1	2.18	3.75	2.09	1.65	5.03
Manual labour	1.51	1.65	1.32	1.49	2.42	3.04	2.12	3.08	1.96	1.69	4.95
Ex-post 2 – base											
Capital	0.02	0.7	0.1	0.64	2.99	4.29	2.47	4.22	2.63	0.72	7.41
Non-manual labour	-0.18	0.6	-0.07	0.24	1.86	3.05	1.78	2.96	1.66	0.43	5.52
Manual labour	0.13	0.76	0.27	0.21	2.74	3.96	2.18	3.84	1.82	0.87	7.46
Wages fixed											
Capital	0.48	0.86	0.56	0.88	1.66	2.29	1.64	2.73	1.64	0.95	4.33
Non-manual labour	0.43	0.95	0.55	0.81	1.54	2.26	1.58	2.78	1.59	0.98	4.48
Manual labour	0.67	0.97	0.74	0.73	1.65	2.26	1.53	2.37	1.4	1.13	4.44

Comparing the results of the base simulation with the outcome when wages are held fixed shows the effects of factor market adjustment. Comparing the two ex-post 1 simulations, the effect of the SMP seems to be to increase the demand for non-manual labour relative to manual labour: the effect of wage adjustment is to dampen relative demand for non-manual labour. This is particularly clear in the four large EU economies and in Spain, where factor price adjustment decreases the demand for non-manual labour and raises the demand for manual labour; but for the other economies, although the demand for non-manual labour increases, it generally does so by less than the demand for manual labour. What is striking about the ex-post 2 simulations is how much smaller the factor market impact is. Modelling the SMP as liberalizing external trade in manufacturing sectors as well as intra-EU trade implies much less expansion in factor demands in manufacturing, though the direction of the relative factor market adjustment is as in the ex-post 1 simulations: now the demand for both manual and non-manual labour is dampened in the five large economies, increased in the smaller economies, but in all cases the relative demand for non-manual labour is reduced by factor market adjustment.

5.9. Interpretation of the results and comparison with the econometric results

It would be desirable to provide a full integration of the econometric and CGE methodologies, by using the econometric estimates of the effects of the SMP as the input into the CGE model. However, a full comparison of CGE results with econometric results is not possible, because the econometric analysis covers only a limited range of sectors, and some of those are sectors where the CGE has had to operate at a more aggregated level because of data constraints. There are in fact 11 sectors in which a comparison is possible, and details are given in unpublished Appendix Table A5.5. Table 5.8 shows the results at the aggregate level.

Table 5.8.   Comparison of econometric and CGE results, all manufacturing

Market shares	Home	EU	RoW	Change in p-c margin
Base (1991)	68.2	23.0	8.8	
Changes				
Actual 91-94	-2.8	0.3	2.5	
Econometric				
Direct	-2.2	0.5	1.7	
Competition	-0.1	0.0	0.1	-3.6
Total	-2.3	0.5	1.8	
CGE				
BIL [1990]	-2.3	2.8	-0.5	
Ex-post 1 total	-1.5	1.8	-0.3	
Ex-post 1 competition	0.0	0.0	0.0	
Ex-post 2 total	-2.9	1.8	1.1	
Ex-post 2 competition	0.1	0.0	0.0	
Ex-post 1 integrated markets	-1.2	2.4	-1.2	

The base market shares are those for 1991, the base year from which both models calculate changes in import penetration, averaged across the four large economies. The econometric results, as in Chapter 4, are similarly reported as the average for these four countries, divided as before, between direct and competition effects. The CGE results reported are the market share effects produced by the ex-ante simulation based on BIL [1990], the two ex-post simulations, with the competition effects in each also identified, and finally the first ex-post simulation with the assumption of integrated markets. The two ex-post simulations are designed to reproduce the change in the market share of intra-EU imports, but averaged across all EU markets, and furthermore the CGE simulations were done on data in which post-1993 intra-EU trade was increased by 10% to allow for the INTRASTAT problem, so the 1.8% increase shown in the ex-post simulation is not equal to the 0.3% increase reported above as the actual change in intra-EU market shares.

Unsurprisingly, the econometric analysis does a better job of tracking the actual changes in trade shares than do the CGE simulations. The fact that even the second ex-post simulation, in which the reduction in extra-EU trade costs was modelled as being equal to the reduction in intra-EU trade cost, fails to track the actual growth of extra-EU imports confirms the econometric results which imply external effects which are stronger than internal ones. Given that the different forms of analysis have different strengths, it is particularly interesting that both the econometric and the CGE analyses imply that the liberalization of external trade has been at least as strong as the intra-EU liberalizing effects of the SMP. This could be interpreted as the SMP having caused external liberalization, perhaps because of the market access effects of having a single regulatory system, or explicit rules about public procurement. Alternatively, it could be interpreted as the SMP having been accompanied by external liberalization. In either event, it is clear that concerns about 'fortress Europe' effects of the SMP were unnecessary: the SMP has not in itself closed the EU market to third countries, nor has it been accompanied by protectionist measures.

It is interesting that in some of the sectors in which the actual market shares move in a counter-intuitive way, the econometric estimates of the effects of the SMP have the expected signs, so the conditioning variables are succeeding in explaining the apparently anomalous data. Thus we have another conclusion: where intra-EU trade seems to have declined, the fall is likely to be largely the result of other economic forces, rather than of perverse effects from the SMP.

The most interesting comparison between the two methodologies is in the comparison of the size of the competition effects that the different approaches obtain. The definition of the competition effect is the same in both approaches, being the effect of changing price-cost margins, with both factor prices and scale effects taken account of on the cost side in both models. The sectoral tables in the unpublished Appendix Table A5.5 allow a comparison to be made in 7 of the 11 sectors (in the remaining 4, because of a falling share of intra-EU imports, the ex-post simulations set the SMP effect at zero). In these cases there is a very clear pattern: the competition effects in the econometric estimates are typically of the order of 30% or more of the direct effects, while the CGE model simulates the competition effects as being typically less, often much less, than 10% of the direct effects of the SMP. This is an important conclusion given the role that CGE-type models have been given in recent years in estimating economy-wide impacts of trade policy reform – even a model which places imperfect competition at its heart seems to underestimate the true competition effects of the SMP. If this conclusion were borne out by more systematic investigation than has been possible in the present project, it would have important implications for future work.

5.10. Conclusions

We can draw the principal conclusions of the CGE simulations as follows:

(a)   the sectoral distribution of the effects of the SMP appears to have been significantly different from that predicted in 1990;

(b)   there seem to have been liberalizing forces on external trade that are at least as strong as the intra-EU effects of the SMP;

(c)   the competition effects of the SMP may be much more substantial than those incorporated in standard models of imperfect competition.

6. Conclusions

Our analysis in this study has been based on three complementary approaches: descriptive statistics, econometric modelling, and computable general equilibrium (CGE) simulation.

Our principal conclusions are:

(a)   Given the multiplicity of influences on trade performance, it is impossible to get satisfactory statistical evidence on 'competitiveness' from trade patterns, and we have concentrated on the less ambitious task of obtaining evidence of the impact of the SMP on 'competition'.

(b)   The different experiences of different countries suggest that there have been changes in competitiveness which cannot be attributed solely to exchange rate effects or to other macroeconomic influences.

(c)   Inter-sectoral differences within countries are similarly sufficiently large to imply that there were microeconomic, sectoral influences on competitiveness, as well as exchange rate and other macroeconomic factors.

(d)   There seems little evidence of common patterns of changes in sectoral competitiveness across countries, except in sectors where the changes seem to derive from long-run structural change, independent of the SMP.

(e)   Market share analysis provides clear evidence that the change in the measurement of intra-EU trade in 1993 has had quite a strong effect on the statistics.

(f)   In most sectors, EU markets have become increasingly open to imports from the rest of the world, with changes in the 1990s being the continuation of a longer-run trend.

(g)   Several sectors show an increasing pace of extra-EU import penetration, so either the SMP or other changes in the 1990s have increased the openness of markets to extra-EU imports as well as intra-EU imports.

(h)   Econometric estimates suggest that the direct demand impact of the SMP reduced domestic market shares by 5.4% on average in the 15 sensitive sectors and by 2.2% in manufacturing as a whole. EU and Rest of the World producers are estimated to have both gained from the SMP, roughly in the same proportion. A similar pattern is repeated throughout the industries studied.

(i)   The single market measures have also been found to have improved price competition and reduced price-cost margins. We estimate that the SMP has compressed price-cost margins by 3.9% on average in the 15 sensitive sectors and by 3.6% in manufacturing as a whole. This behaviour is reflected generally amongst industries.

(j)   In the 15 'sensitive' sectors for which econometric estimates were derived, on average improved price-cost margins are estimated to have restored domestic market shares by 1.2%, roughly a quarter of our estimate of the reduction caused by direct demand-side effects. The simulation results demonstrate that it is essential to consider the supply-side effects of the SMP on increasing competition to obtain a full evaluation of the programme.

(k)   Our estimates of the overall impact of the SMP taking into account both demand and competition effects, suggest that the programme has been strongly trade creating. The overall impact on domestic market shares is estimated to have been 4.2% in the 15 sensitive sectors and 2.3% in manufacturing as a whole.

(l)   It is also clear that there is little evidence of trade diversion. The overall impact of the SMP is estimated to have increased extra-EU import shares by 2.0% in the 15 sensitive sectors and by 1.8% in overall manufacturing.

(m)   Comparison of different CGE simulations shows that there have been more influences on the trade pattern than a simple reduction in intra-EU barriers.

(n)   The sectoral distribution of the effects of the SMP has been quite different from that expected in advance of the implementation of the programme.

(o)   The CGE analysis confirms the conclusion of the econometric estimates that there have been liberalizing forces on external trade that are at least as strong as the intra-EU effects of the SMP.

(p)   Concerns about 'fortress Europe' effects of the SMP were unnecessary: the SMP has not in itself closed the EU market to third countries, nor has it been accompanied by protectionist measures.

(q)   The competition effects of the SMP may be much more substantial than those incorporated in standard models of imperfect competition.

Technical appendix to Chapter 2

A.2.1. Econometric methodology

A.2.1.1. Investigating the effects of the single market on demand

Modelling demand for home and imported goods

We first set up a demand system to represent consumer preferences. Goods are assumed to be differentiated by place of production. Consumers allocate their demand for the different countries' goods depending on relative prices and real expenditure in the sector in question. We assume that the system of consumer preferences themselves are unaffected by the SMP.

We use the 'almost ideal demand' system of Deaton and Muellbauer [1980]. This allows the constraints of rational behaviour to be imposed through a set of parameter restrictions. This ensures that the model is consistent with utility maximization, helping the interpretation of the results and potentially allowing for welfare comparisons to be made. It provides a second order approximation to any underlying cost function and is widely used in demand analysis. The resultant cross-equation restrictions also improve the efficiency of our estimation.

We can write the 'almost ideal demand' system results in the form of the following set of market demand shares for each industry:

$$s_{ik} = \alpha_i + \sum_j \gamma_{ij} \ln p_{jk} + \beta_i \ln Y_k / P_k \tag{1}$$

where s_{ik} is the budget share of the ith country supplier in the kth country's market and p_{jk} is the price of the jth country supplier into the kth country market. Y_k is total nominal expenditure by k residents, and P_k is a price index covering supplies from all sources.

The adding up of the demand shares imposes the following restrictions on the parameters:

$$\sum_i \alpha_i = 1 ; \quad \sum_i \gamma_{ij} = \sum_i \beta_i = 0 \tag{2}$$

which will automatically be satisfied since the demand shares in the data add to unity.

The demand functions must be homogeneous of degree zero in prices which entails the further restrictions that:

$$\sum_j \gamma_{ij} = 0 \tag{3}$$

Slutsky symmetry further requires:

$$\gamma_{ij} = \gamma_{ji} \tag{4}$$

Global negativity of substitution can only be imposed in the 'almost ideal demand' system at the cost of severe restrictions on the possible range of price elasticities (Diewert and Wales [1987]). We therefore impose negativity on our estimates only if necessary.

Modelling the effects of integration on import prices

The SMP can have two effects on import prices: the direct effect of the SMP measures in reducing both the transport and administrative costs of trading across frontiers; and the impact of increased competitiveness within markets on price-cost mark-ups. We model both of these effects by examining the behaviour of the mark-up of prices of importer firms relative to the prices they charge within their own domestic market.

We can write the typical equation for the import price of the *j*th country's products into the *k*th market as:

$$\ln p_{jk} = \ln p_{jj} + \eta_{jk} + \tau_{jk} \tag{5}$$

where p_{jj} is the producer's price in its home market, η_{jk} is the mark-up of prices to the *k*th market over the price of domestic supplies to the home market prior to the SMP measures. τ_{jk} is a dummy variable which measures the change in this mark-up as a result of the SMP.

In our empirical estimates we allow a dummy variable in our dynamic equations for each year from 1992 onwards. The overall SMP impact is then determined by evaluating the permanent effect on market shares.

The reduced form demand system model

In principle, both sets of structural equations (1) and (5) could be estimated individually. Owing to the difficulty of obtaining good quality bilateral import price data however, we have chosen to estimate the reduced form of the system.

Substituting the import price equations (5) in the set of demand share equations (1), we obtain the reduced form for the *i*th budget share in the *k*th country:

$$s = \alpha_i + \sum_{j \neq k} \gamma_{ij} \cdot (\eta_{jk} + \tau_{jk}) + \sum_j \gamma_{ij} \cdot \ln p_{jj} + \beta_i \ln Y_k / P_k \tag{6}$$

This set of reduced form demand equations continues to inherit the properties of rationality of the original set of equations (1) under the same set of restrictions as discussed above. In particular, the system still adds up, since:

$$\sum_i \gamma_{ij} \cdot (\eta_{jk} + \tau_{jk}) = 0.$$

Note that we are unable to individually identify the parameters η_{jk} and τ_{jk}. The η_{jk} terms are incorporated into the constants of the equations. The SMP dummy terms τ_{jk} form new composite dummy variables in each of the reduced form demand equations,

$$\tau_i^k = \sum_{j \neq k} \gamma_{ij} \cdot \tau_{jk}$$

A.2.1.2. Modelling the effects of the single market on improved supply performance

Our approach to modelling the impact of the SMP on supply performance and domestic prices is based on modelling the determination of domestic prices within an explicit oligopoly setting. Domestic firms are assumed to compete in price strategies with import competitors: their prices in general will depend on their own costs, their competitors' prices, and the size of their competitors' market share. The IMP can have two supply-side effects: an increase of competition in markets as a result of more competitive import availability, likely to result in the narrowing of the mark-up of price over marginal cost by domestic firms; and the impact of greater exploitation of economies of scale etc., reducing marginal costs themselves.

A structural model is available for application here. In Allen [1994], we have derived an oligopoly model of price competition in an industry where consumer demands are given by an 'almost ideal demand' system. An important feature of this demand system is that market shares themselves affect the elasticity of firm own-price demands. A firm whose market share declines will find itself faced with a more elastic own-price elasticity of demand. Its price-cost margin will thus be forced to narrow.

Allen shows how the model results in log-linear reaction functions, in which a firm's price is a log-linear combination of its own costs and possibly its competitor's prices, with parameters dependent on its conjectural variations of the responses of competitors to changes in own policies.

We specify the technology of firms in country j by a Cobb-Douglas cost function:

$$c_j = \frac{1}{1+\delta} w_j^\alpha m_j^{1-\alpha} y_j^{1+\delta} \tag{7}$$

where c_j is total costs, w_j is unit labour costs, m_j the costs of other inputs, and y_j the output of the industry. The parameter δ is a measure of the returns to scale.

Marginal costs are then given by:

$$c_j' = w_j^\alpha m_j^{1-\alpha} y_j^\delta \tag{8}$$

We have examined a very general specification for the price equation. In general prices are a mark-up on both domestic marginal costs and competitor import prices:

$$\ln p_{jj} = \mu_j(\alpha \ln w_j + (1-\alpha)\ln m_j + \delta \ln(y_j))$$
$$+ (1-\mu_j)\sum_{i \neq j} \zeta_{ij} \ln p_{ij} + \varepsilon_j + o_j \tag{9}$$

Domestic prices are therefore a weighted average (with parameter μ_j) of domestic marginal costs and competing importer prices. The parameters ζ_{ij} are a set of weights on importer's prices. They can in principle be explicitly derived from the parameters of the demand function (see Allen [1994]). The term ε_j is the mark-up prior to the SMP and σ_j is a dummy representing the effects of the measure themselves on the mark-up. In our empirical work we again make the substitution of importer prices in terms of foreign domestic prices.

A.2.1.3. Evaluating the overall impact of the single market: *Monde* and *Antimonde*

To evaluate the overall impact of the SMP legislation on trade flows in the European Union we integrate the analyses of Sections A.2.1.1 and A.2.1.2 and derive from our estimated equations the simulations which are presented in Chapter 4.

Conventional measures of the market integration effects consider only the demand effects on trade flows. Within our system of equations these are measured by the composite dummy variables τ_i^k which are estimated within our reduced form demand equations (equation (6)). These give us for each country and product category measures of the impact of lower import costs on domestic consumption of home goods and changes in intra- and extra-EU imports.

Such estimates ignore the supply-side effects of the SMP which work to reduce domestic price-cost margins by increasing competition. In our analysis we have attempted to measure these effects through a further set of dummy variables, σ_j, which are estimated as part of the set of domestic price equations (equation (9)). These dummy variables tell us for each country and product category how domestic prices have been affected by the SMP.

Ignoring these supply-side effects would potentially seriously bias downwards the estimates of the full impact of the SMP measures on trade flows. Given that firms will normally be operating on the elastic part of their demand curves, these domestic price reductions will tend, to some extent, to restore domestic loss of market share. This effect will therefore partially counteract the direct trade creation effects of the SMP. On average, the share of EU producers should rise at the expense of non-EU producers. The extent to which the rise in EU producer share is distributed between increased domestic share or EU imports depends on whether the most affected countries are net importers or exporters and on the exact set of trade price elasticities.

To derive the full impact of the SMP on both demand and supply, we therefore simulate the set of estimated demand equations (6) using the domestic price series for home and EU competitor countries adjusted for the dummies estimated in equation (9). The results give us the additional impact of the supply-side effects on trade flows.

Schematically, we can write the derivation of these full effects (or *Antimonde*) as follows. We can write the equation for the *i*th demand shares in actual world in terms of the *Antimonde* share as:

$$s_i^M = s_i^A + \sum_j \gamma_{ij} [\ln(p_j^{AM}) - \ln(p_j^A)] + dum_i$$

Where the superscripts M and A represent the *Monde* and *Antimonde* cases respectively and dum_i is the estimated SMP demand dummy variable. To derive the *Antimonde* therefore we have to correct both for the direct demand effects of the SMP and differences in prices as a result of the implementation of the SMP.

Examining the determination of prices (and neglecting for simplicity the complications of the influence of competitors' prices on domestic prices), the relationship between prices in the *Monde* and *Antimonde* can be written for the *j*th price as:

$$\ln p_j^M = \ln p_j^A + dump_j$$

where $dump_j$ is the estimated dummy variable in the jth price equation. To evaluate the trade shares in the full *Antimonde*, we must substitute out the effects of the SMP on prices as they would have been if the SMP had not been implemented.

$$s_i^A = s_i^M - [\sum_j \gamma_{ij} dump_j + dum_i$$

We are thus be able to derive for each country and product category estimates of the full effects of the SMP measures on home consumption and intra- and extra-EU trade flows. The full effect can be decomposed into the impact of the conventionally estimated import price effects on demand and also the additional supply-side effects of increased competitiveness.

A.2.2. Computable general equilibrium modelling methodology

Consider first final demand. p_{ij}^k and x_{ij}^k denote the price and quantity of a single product variety of industry k produced in country i and used (as a final demand) in country j. (There are $n_i^k m_i^k$ such varieties, and, because of symmetry, we do not need to introduce a notation for individual varieties.) We follow Dixit and Stiglitz [1977] in assuming consumer preferences with the following two-stage aggregation property. First, varieties within an industry and country of sale aggregate into a quantity index X_j^k with associated price index P_j^k. The aggregator function has constant elasticity of substitution (common to all countries) denoted ε^k. Aggregation is over products from all sources; as contrasted with the Armington assumption of separate nesting of products by geographical source. Second, the price indices, P_j^k, enter the expenditure function of a single representative consumer with homothetic preferences in each country. If u_j is utility, E_j is the unit expenditure function, and M_j is income, then the budget constraint of the country j consumer is,

$$M_j = u_j E_j(...,P_j^k,...) \tag{1}$$

E_j is assumed to be Cobb-Douglas. Consumer demands both for the aggregate quantity indices and for individual varieties are derived by partial differentiation of the expenditure function.

The quantity of a single product variety of industry k produced in i and used as an intermediate good in j is denoted y_{ij}^k with price q_{ij}^k. There is two-stage aggregation of intermediates, analogous to that for final products. First, varieties within an industry and country of sale are aggregated into a quantity index Y_j^k with associated price index Q_j^k (again, not separately nested by geographical source). Second, in each country the quantity indices are aggregated into a composite intermediate commodity whose price index in country j is F_j. This implies that there is a single composite intermediate commodity, so that the proportions in which each industry uses the products of other industries are assumed to be the same.

The costs of a firm in industry k of country i are given by a cost function c_i^k,

$$c_i^k = m_i^k \left[h^k (z_i^k) G_i^k (w_i^1, w_i^2, w_i^3) \right] \tag{2}$$

$$\text{where } z_i^k = \sum_j \left[x_{ij}^k + y_{ij}^k \right] \tag{3}$$

z_i^k is the total output per variety of a country i firm in industry k. The function h^k describes the returns to scale in industry k. Increasing returns to scale means that $h^k(z_i^k)/z_i^k$ is decreasing in z_i^k, and we employ a functional form for h^k that permits decreasing marginal cost as well as decreasing average cost. Notice that this function is not country specific. Furthermore, there are no economies of scope, since c_i^k is linear in m_i^k, and returns to scale are associated with output per variety z_i^k. The function G_i^k aggregates input prices into cost per unit h. Its arguments are the intermediate price index, F_j, and factor prices, w_i^l. The functions G_i^k differ by country, but only by a scalar, implying Hicks neutral technical differences. Input demands, which in equilibrium equal factor supplies, v_i^l, are partial derivatives of these cost functions so we have

$$v_i^l = \sum_k n_i^k m_i^k h^k (z_i^k) \frac{\partial G_i^k (F_i, w_i^1, w_i^2, w_i^3)}{\partial w_i^l} \qquad (l=1,..,3) \tag{4}$$

The profits of firms are given by

$$\pi_i^k = m_i^k \sum_j \left[p_{ij}^k x_{ij}^k + q_{ij}^k y_{ij}^k \right] \left[1 - \tau_{ij}^k \right] - t_{ij}^k \left[x_{ij}^k + y_{ij}^k \right] - c_i^k \tag{5}$$

where τ_{ij}^k and t_{ij}^k are respectively the *ad valorem* tariff and transaction costs of shipping a unit of industry k output from economy i to economy j.

We assume that firms act as quantity competitors in segmented markets. Each firm in industry k and country i then chooses sales in market j, x_{ij}^k, taking as constant the sales of all its rivals in each market. Optimization requires the equation of marginal revenue to marginal cost in each market, where the slope of each firm's perceived demand curve depends on the extent of product differentiation, and on the share of the firm in that market. Firms' choice of intermediate sales quantities, y_{ij}^k, is less straightforward. It is possible that purchasers of inputs have some monopsony power, to be combined with the monopoly power of sellers. Further, and perhaps more importantly, even if purchasers of intermediates are input price takers, the demand for intermediates is a derived demand, and establishing the elasticity of the derived demand curve is not straightforward. For these reasons we assume that the price of a good sold as an intermediate equals the price of the same good sold to final demand. Furthermore, the number of varieties of intermediate goods entering the price indices Q_j^k is held constant, so abstracting from any variety effects on the users of intermediate goods.

All that remains to complete the description of the model is the determination of income. Income accruing to factor l in economy i is $w_i^l v_i^l$. National income is factor income accruing to the three factors, plus the profits of firms and CET revenue.

Technical appendix to Chapter 4

A.4.1. Econometric and statistical issues in estimation

A.4.1.1. Econometric estimation of the demand equations

Estimation methodology

In our estimation of the demand equations we are faced with very small sample sizes. We typically have just 18 observations from 1976 to 1994 on the five core countries (Germany, France, Italy, the UK, and Belgium) and 14 observations from 1980 to 1994 for the other countries. In the circumstances it is important to obtain the most efficient possible estimates.

For the estimation we have used maximum likelihood, estimating the full set of equations together. We have estimated a full covariance matrix, since we have relatively low dimensionality, and the use of a misspecified model would be worse.

Our initial estimates were of the partial adjustment system with a diagonalized adjustment matrix. The requirements of consumer theory, homogeneity and symmetry were imposed to ensure the efficiency of the estimates. Time trends were initially excluded from the estimates. This was the maximal feasible estimating system given the small sample of data constraints.

The econometric specification of the demand equations

In our empirical work, we have found that a partial adjustment mechanism was adequate to characterize all the empirical dynamics. A partial adjustment mechanism would be compatible with quadratic adjustment costs or more generally may represent a general dynamic form.

We write the general partial adjustment formulation of the demand share equations in the form:

$$\Delta S_t = K(S_t^* - S_{t-1}) + \varepsilon_t \tag{1}$$

where ε_t is an $nx1$ vector of error terms.

The optimal shares are given by equation (6) in the Appendix to Chapter 2, which can be written in the matrix form:

$$S_t^* = A.x_t \tag{2}$$

where x_t is the vector $[1, \ln p_{1k_t}, .. , \ln p_{ik_t}, .., \ln p_{nk_t}, \ln Y_t / P_t]$.

The demand share equations can then be written as:

$$\Delta S_t = K.(A.x_t - S_{t-1}) + \varepsilon_t \tag{3}$$

It is well known that the parameters of the K matrix are not all empirically identified, because of the adding up property of the shares (see Berndt and Savin [1975], Anderson and Blundell [1982], and Allen and Urga [1995]). We thus define a new $nxn-1$ matrix K^*, whose elements are defined as $k_{ij}^* = k_{ij} - k$. Likewise, we define A^n as the A matrix minus the nth row and the S_t^n as the vector of shares minus the nth row.

We can now define our estimating equations as:

$$\Delta S_t = K^* . (A^n . x_t - S_{t-1}^n) + \varepsilon_t \tag{4}$$

Because of the singularity in the error terms, in our estimation procedure, we drop the nth equation. The parameters of this equation can be fully derived from those of the other estimated equations (see Anderson and Blundell [1982]).

Tests of conditioning

Our first priority was to obtain a validly conditioned set of estimates so as to make further inference possible. To this end, we have undertaken a comprehensive examination of the properties of the residuals of our equations. We have tested our estimated residuals for autocorrelation, autoregressive conditional heteroscedasticity (ARCH), and normality. To test the properties of the system as a whole we have also carried out these tests on the derived residuals of the implicit third equation.

The autocorrelation test is the small-sample modified portmanteau statistic suggested by Ljung and Box [1978]. This has reasonable properties in small samples. The statistic is calculated as:

$$Q^* = T.(T+2).\sum_{\tau=1}^{P} (T-\tau)^{-1} . r^2(\tau) \tag{5}$$

where T is the length of the sample period, P is the number of autocorrelations considered, and $r^2(\tau)$ is the square of the autocorrelation coefficient of the residuals at lag τ. The statistic is distributed as $\chi^2(P)$. First-order statistics are reported in the tables.

The test of autoregressive conditional heteroscedasticity (ARCH) is that suggested by Engel [1982]. We have again used the Ljung-Box small-sample correction. First-order ARCH statistics are also reported in the tables.

Finally, we have tested for normality of the residuals using the Jarque-Bera [1980] test. This tests for skewness and kurtosis of the residuals and is distributed $\chi^2(2)$.

In most cases the presence of the lagged dynamic terms was enough to eliminate autocorrelated and ARCH processes; in some countries however, there was clear evidence of non-normality, usually caused by significant outliers. We have augmented such equation systems with additional dummy variables. A full list of such dummies is included in the Appendix tables (unpublished).

Some attention has also been paid to the dynamic specification of the equations. Where the estimated adjustment coefficient was greater than unity, the coefficient has been imposed as unity, effectively resulting in a static formulation of the system. The foregoing battery of tests was then further applied to the resultant static equations.

Testing and imposing negativity

To improve efficiency, we have imposed price homogeneity and symmetry on the demand functions. For our equations to be valid representations of a demand system, we also require that they obey the Slutsky negativity condition on their implicit substitution matrix.

The practical implications of this are important. Satisfaction of negativity ensures that all own-price compensated elasticities are non-positive. This is clearly essential in order to derive sensible estimates of the impact of the SMP.

Slutsky negativity entails that the substitution matrix of Hicksian elasticities of substitution is negative semi-definite. That matrix consists of the terms:

$$\{ \sigma_{ij} \} = \frac{1}{s_i . s_j} . [\gamma_{ij} - s_i . \delta_{ij} + s_i . s_j + \beta_i . \beta_j . \ln Y / P] \qquad (6)$$

Sufficient conditions for imposing global negativity in the 'almost ideal demand' system exist only in the homothetic case. Even then the imposition of Slutsky negativity on equation estimates puts potentially unacceptable *a priori* constraints on the set of possible elasticities of substitution.

We have therefore not imposed global negativity on our initial set of estimates. Instead, we have examined the eigenvalues of the estimated Slutsky substitution matrix to check for conformity. Where negativity has been violated at 1990 base year values, we have imposed that the price coefficient matrix is negative semi-definite.[2]

To impose negativity, we have used a technique introduced in production analysis by Diewert and Wales [1987], drawing on Wiley, Schmidt, and Bramble [1973]. The matrix of price coefficients is factorized as follows:

$$\Gamma = - T.T' \qquad (7)$$

where Γ is the *{n-1}x{n-1}* matrix of price coefficients and T is a lower triangular matrix of the same dimension.

The resultant equation system is highly non-linear in parameters. We have therefore used the quasi-Newton algorithm of Davidson-Fletcher-Powell to solve the optimization problem. This technique generally has good convergence properties for extremely non-linear problems.

In the tables we have reported both the set of eigenvalues of the substitution matrix in 1990 and the set of own-price *un*compensated or Marshallian elasticities.

---

[2]   Cooper *et al.* [1992] note that global negativity cannot be imposed in the 'almost ideal demand' system and suggest that the Engel curve effects may be misspecified. In the circumstances it seems reasonable to ensure negativity at least regionally in the range of observations of interest. Choosing the 1990 base year as a criterion for negativity ensures that the system obeys negativity over the most recent period.

A.4.1.2. Econometric estimation of the domestic price equations

Estimation methodology

In estimating the set of price equations, we have again been faced with very small sample sizes of 18 or 14 years. We have again therefore employed the most efficient and parsimonious estimation techniques. For our final estimates, we have used iterative non-linear SURE to estimate the set of different country equations for each sector simultaneously.

In the estimation of the price equations there is the additional problem of clearly non-stationary data. Cointegration tests lack power in very small samples of time averaged data (see Hague [1995]). In order to select our regressors, preliminary testing for cointegrating relationships was undertaken using both Engle-Granger and Johansen procedures. Unfortunately, this analysis could only be taken as a guide, since the power of the tests to reject the null of a unit root is extremely small.

Conditional on cointegration, inference can be made on the basis of standard chi-squared likelihood ratio tests. In the tables we have quoted standard t-statistics which are valid on the assumption of cointegration.

The econometric specification of the price equations

Again to preserve degrees of freedom we have adopted a partial adjustment formulation of the price equations. In order to increase the efficiency of our estimates, price homogeneity has been imposed.

The partial adjustment formulation can be written as:

$$\Delta \ln p_{jj} = \lambda_j (\ln p_{jj}^* - \ln p_{jjt-1})$$ (8)

where p_{jj}^* is the underlying equilibrium price given by equation (9) (p. 77) and λ_j is an adjustment parameter.

Bibliography

Allen, C.B. 'An empirical model of pricing, market share, and market conduct', Sussex University Discussion Paper 10/94, 1994, forthcoming in *Manchester School*.

Allen, C.B. and Urga, G. 'Derivation and estimation of interrelated factor demands from a dynamic cost function', Centre for Economic Forecasting Discussion Paper DP 10-95, 1995, London Business School.

Anderson, G.J. and Blundell, R.W. 'Estimation and hypothesis testing in dynamic single equation systems', *Econometrica* **50**, 1982, 1559-1571.

Baldwin, R.E. 'The growth effects of 1992', *Economic Policy* **9**, 1990, 247-281.

Baldwin, R.E., Forslid, R. and Haaland, J. 'Investment creation and investment diversion: simulation analysis of the single market programme', Discussion Paper 1308, Centre for Economic Policy Research, London, December 1995.

Baldwin, R.E. and Venables, A.J. 'Methodologies for the ex-post evaluation of the single European market', unpublished report to DG II, European Commission, 1994.

Baldwin, R.E. and Venables, A.J. 'Regional economic integration', in Grossman, G. and Rogoff, K. (eds) *Handbook of International Economics*, Vol. 3. North-Holland, Amsterdam, 1995.

Ben David, D. 'Equalizing exchange: trade liberalization and economic convergence', *Quarterly Journal of Economics*, August 1993.

Berndt, E.R. and Savin, N.E. 'Estimation and hypothesis testing in singular equation systems with autoregressive errors', *Econometrica* **43**, 1975, 937-958.

de Boer, P.M.C., Martínez, C. and Harkena, R. 'Imports of manufactures and Spain's accession to the European Union', Paper given at World Congress of Econometric Society, Tokyo, 1995.

Brenton, P.A. and Winters, L.A. 'Bilateral trade elasticities for exploring the effects of 1992', in L.A. Winters (ed) *Trade Flows and Trade Policy After '1992'*, Cambridge, Cambridge University Press/Centre for Economic Policy Research, 1992.

Buigues, P., Ilzkovitz, F. and Lebrun, J.-F. [BIL] (1990) 'The impact of the internal market by industrial sector: the challenge for the Member States', *European Economy*, Special Issue, Luxembourg, Office for Official Publications of the EC.

Cooper, R.J. and McLaren, K.R. 'A system of demand equations with effectively global regularity conditions'. University of Western Sydney Working Paper 92/06, 1992.

Cox, D. and Harris, R. 'Trade liberalization and industrial organization: some estimates for Canada', *Journal of Political Economy*, 1985.

Davies, S. and Lyons, B. (eds), *Industrial Organization in the European EU*, Oxford, Oxford University Press, 1996.

Deaton, A. and Muellbauer, J.N.J. 'An 'almost ideal demand' system', *American Economic Review* **113**, 1980, 3-25.

Diewert, W.E. and Wales, T. 'Flexible functional forms and global curvature conditions', *Econometrica* **55**, 1, 1987, 43-68.

Dixit, A.K. and Stiglitz, J.E. 'Monopolistic competition and optimum product diversity', *American Economic Review* **67**, 1977, 297-308.

Emerson, M. *et al.* 'The economics of 1992', *European Economy*, No. 35, March 1988, Luxembourg, Office for Official Publications of the EC.

Engel, R.F. 'A general approach to Lagrange multiplier model diagnostics', *Journal of Econometrics* **20**, 1, 1982, 83-104.

European Commission, Directorate-General for Economic and Financial Affairs. 'The impact of exchange rate movements on trade within the single market', *European Economy, Reports and Studies*, No. 4, 1995, Luxembourg, Office for Official Publications of the EC.

Gasiorek, M., Smith, A. and Venables, A.J. '"1992": trade, factor prices and welfare in general equilibrium', in Winters (1992), 35-63.

Hague, A.A. 'The power of cointegration tests: does the frequency of observation matter?' mimeo, York University, Canada, presented at 7th World Congress of the Econometric Society, 1995.

Helpman, E. and Krugman, P.R. *Market Structure and Foreign Trade*, Cambridge, Mass., MIT Press, 1985.

Jacquemin, A. and Sapir, A. 'Competition and imports in the European market' in Winters, L.A. and Venables, A.J. (eds.) *European Integration: Trade and Industry*, Cambridge, Cambridge University Press and CEPR, 1991.

Jarque, C.M. and Bera, A.K. 'Efficient tests for normality, homoscedasticity and serial independence of regression residuals', *Economics Letters* **6**, 1980, 255-259.

Johnson, H.G. 'The economic theory of customs EUs', Chapter 3 in *Money, Trade and Economic Growth*, London, George Allen and Unwin, 1962, 46-74.

Krugman, P. *Pop Internationalism,* Cambridge, Mass., MIT Press, 1996.

Ljung, G.M. and Box, G.E.P. 'On a measure of lack of fit in time series models', *Biometrica* **66**, 1978, 67-72.

Lucas, Jr., R.E., 'On the mechanics of economic development', *Journal of Monetary Economics* **22**, July 1988, 3-42.

Martínez, C. 'The European EU's competitiveness in the Triad. Methodological issues and analyses of indicators', typescript II/705/95-EN, European Commission, 1996.

Martínez, C. and de Boer, P.M.C. 'Assessing the impact of Spain's accession to the European EU on its imports of manufactures', 1995, forthcoming in *Revista Española de Economica.*

Meade, J.E. *The Theory of Customs Unions*, Amsterdam, North-Holland, 1995.

Pratten, C. 'A survey of the economies of scale', in *Studies on the Economics of Integration, Research on the 'Cost of Non-Europe': Basic Findings*, Vol. 2, European Commission, 1988, Luxembourg, Office for Official Publications of the EC.

Romer, P,M. 'Increasing returns and long-run growth', *Journal of Political Economy* **94**, 1986, 1002-1037.

Sleuwagen, L. and Yamawaki, H. 'The formation of the European Common Market and changes in market structure and performance', *European Economic Review* **32**, 1988, 1451-1475.

Smith, A. and Venables, A.J. 'Completing the internal market in the European Community: some industry simulations', *European Economic Review* **32**, 1988, 1501-1525.

Smith, A. and Venables, A.J. 'Economic integration and market access', *European Economic Review* **35**, 1991, 388-395.

Viner, J. *The Customs EU Issue*, New York, Carnegie Endowment for International Peace, 1950.

Wiley, D.E., Schmidt, W.H. and Bramble, W.J. 'Studies of a class of covariance structure models', *Journal of the American Statistical Association* **68**, 1973, 317-323.

Williamson, K. and Porter, F. 'UK visible trade statistics – the Intrastat system', *Economic Trends*, No. 490, August 1994, 38-49.

Winters, L.A. 'British imports of manufactures and the Common Market', *Oxford Economic Papers* **36**, 1984, 103-118.

Winters, L.A. (ed.) *Trade Flows and Trade Policy after '1992'*, Cambridge, Cambridge University Press and Centre for Economic Policy Research, 1992.